MW01624411

Petit Pattern Book

Petit Pattern Book
Kids & Toys

Published in 2007 by BNN, Inc.
1F 35 Sankyo Bldg., 3-7-2, Irifune
Chuo-ku, Tokyo 104-0042 Japan
info@bnn.co.jp
www.bnn.co.jp

Art Direction: Masanari Nakayama (2m09cmGRAPHICS)
Book Design: Shota Yamagiwa (2m09cmGRAPHICS)
Pattern Design: 2m09cmGRAPHICS
Translation: R.I.C. Publication Asia Co., Inc.

ISBN 978-4-86100-506-0

Printed in Japan by Shinano, Ltd.

おしゃれなパターン素材集

キッズ・トイ

Petit Pattern Book

kids & toys

はじめに

「こんなパターン集がほしかった！」
いままでありそうでなかった、おしゃれな素材集の誕生です。デジタルなのに、なんだか味のあるパターンたち。紙に出力するだけで、とってもかわいいプリントになります。CD-ROMには、Illustrator用EPSファイルとPhotoshop用JPEGファイルで、本に掲載しているすべてのパターンがデータ収録されているので、気に入ったパターンをそのまま使うのはもちろん、色を変えたりサイズを変えたり、あなただけのオリジナルパターンをつくることもできます。お部屋のアクセントにしたり、デイリーの小物をリメイクしたり、大切な人へのプレゼントを包んだり。メインに、背景に、ピンポイントに、パターンを生かした手作りグッズで、日々の暮らしをいっそう楽しく演出しましょう。

Introduction

"At last - the collection of patterns I wanted!"

The collection of stylish patterns, which everyone has been waiting for, is finally available. Although they are digital images they have their own personalities. You can make pretty prints just by outputting on paper. In the CD-ROM provided, EPS files for Illustrator and JPEG files for Photoshop are to be found; because they contain the data for all the patterns in the book, you can not only use any patterns you like as they are, but you can also change colors or sizes, or make your original patterns. You can use them to match the decoration of your room, to remake objects you use everyday, or as paper to wrap presents for people who are important to you. When you make original items, use the patterns to form the main part of your design, as a background, or as a focal point. They will surely liven up your everyday life.

contents

008 パターンをつかったあれこれ
Things you can make with patterns

015 キッズ・トイ　001〜140
Kids & Toys 001-140

157 パターンの使い方（Photoshop＆Illustrator）
How to use patterns（Guide in English starts from p177）

はじめる前に
Before you start

パターンで塗る
Tiling with a pattern

「Illustrator」を使ってパターンの色を変える
How to change the color of a pattern with Illustrator

パターンをデスクトップの壁紙にする
How to use the pattern as a desktop background of your computer

164 パターンをつかってつくるもの
Let's use the patterns to make an original article（p184）

1. ブロックパズルをつくる
How to make a "block puzzle"

2. ミニカレンダーをつくる
How to make a "mini calender"

3. ペンケースをつくる
How to make a "pencase"

170 パターン・インデックス
Index for patterns

175 使用許諾
License Agreement of the Software（p190）

Petit Pattern Book

things you can make with patterns

パターンをつかったあれこれ

Petit Pattern Book
kids & toys

STAEDTLER KARAT
STAEDTLER
Radar

2007 DIARY
petit pattern diary
2007 DIARY
petit pattern diary
2007 DIARY
petit pattern diary

Petit Pattern Shop
domus

Petit Pattern Book

キッズ・トイ

001〜140

Petit Pattern Book

kids & toys

002 キッズ・トイ *kids & toys*

003

キッズ・トイ *kids & toys*

• 005 キッズ・トイ *kids & toys*

006 キッズ・トイ *kids & toys*

007 キッズ・トイ *kids & toys*

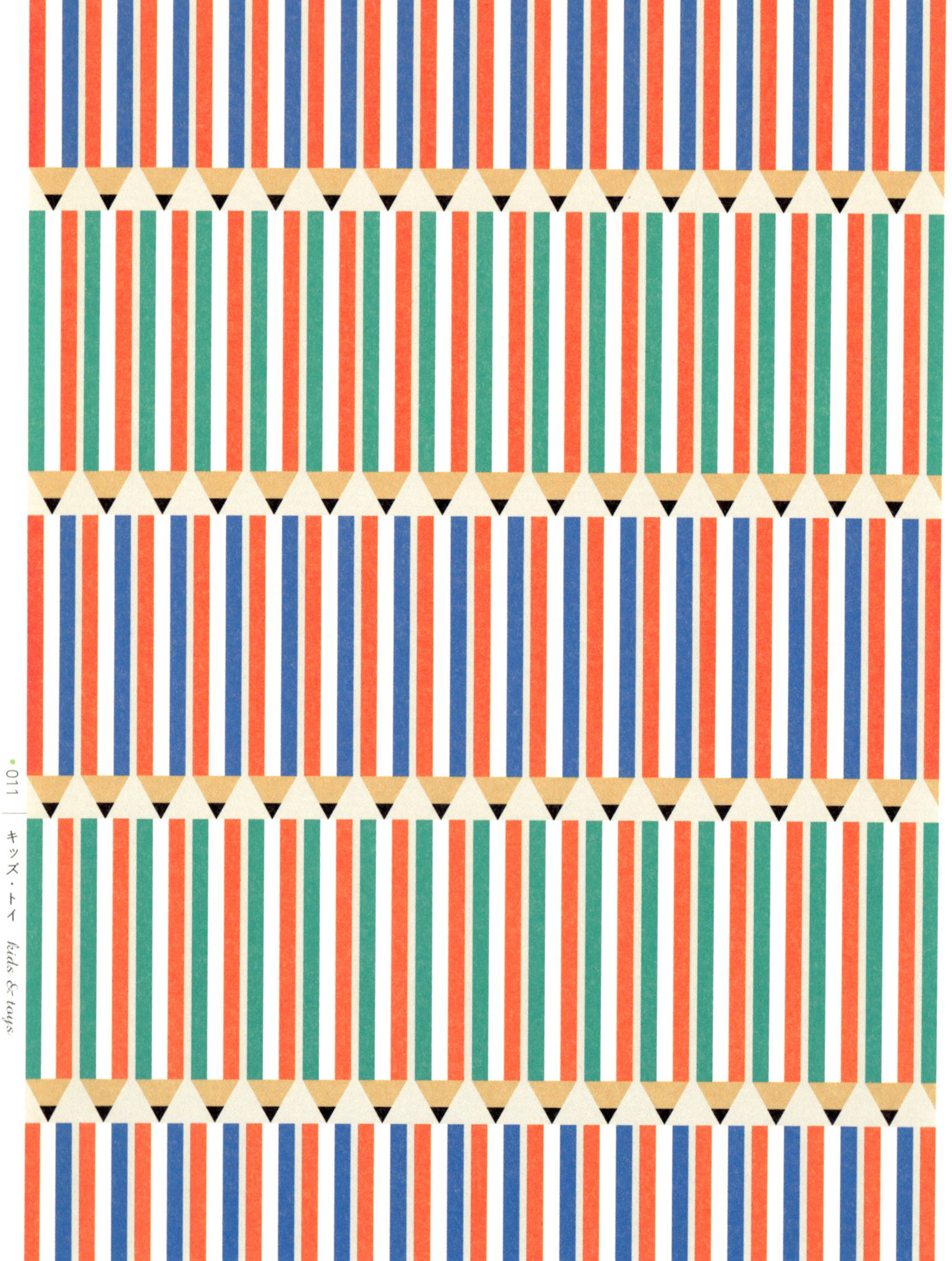

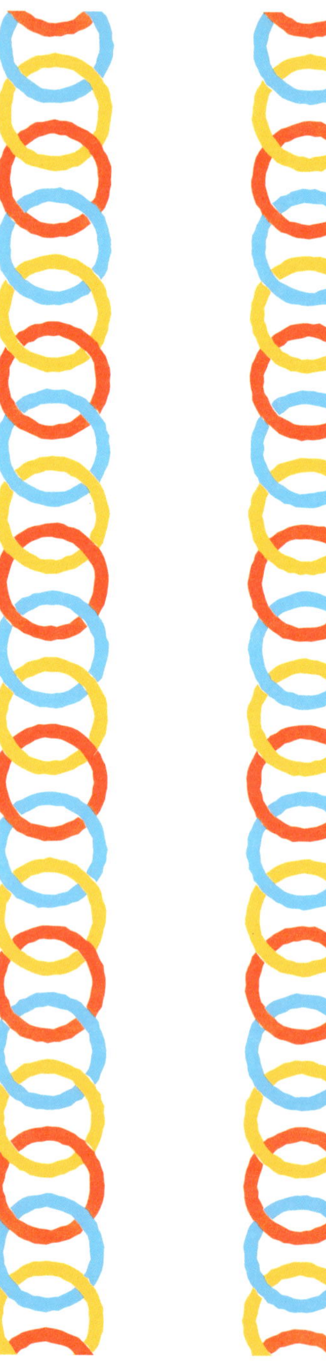

•017 キッズ・トイ *kids & toys*

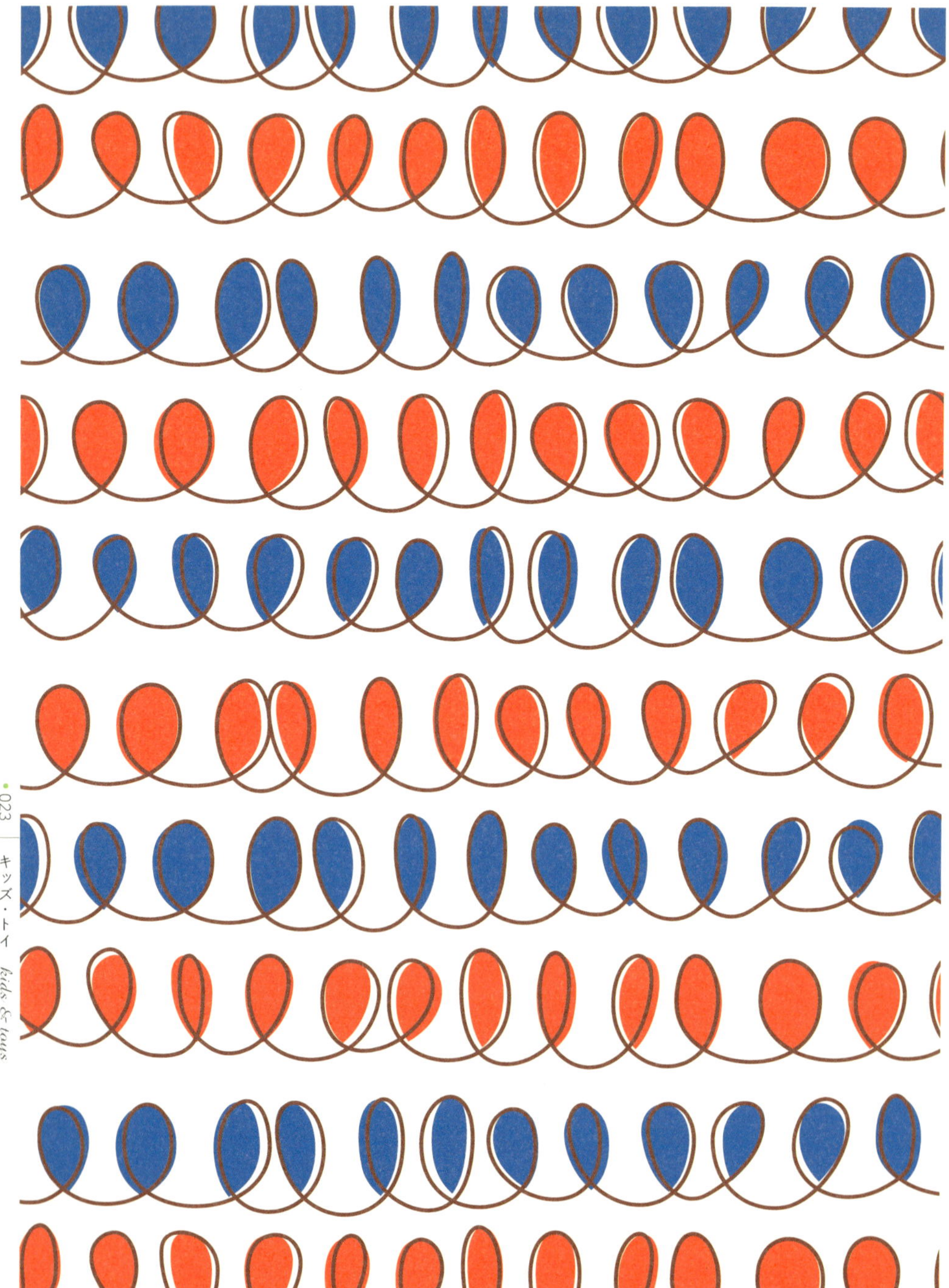

025 キッズ・トイ *kids & toys*

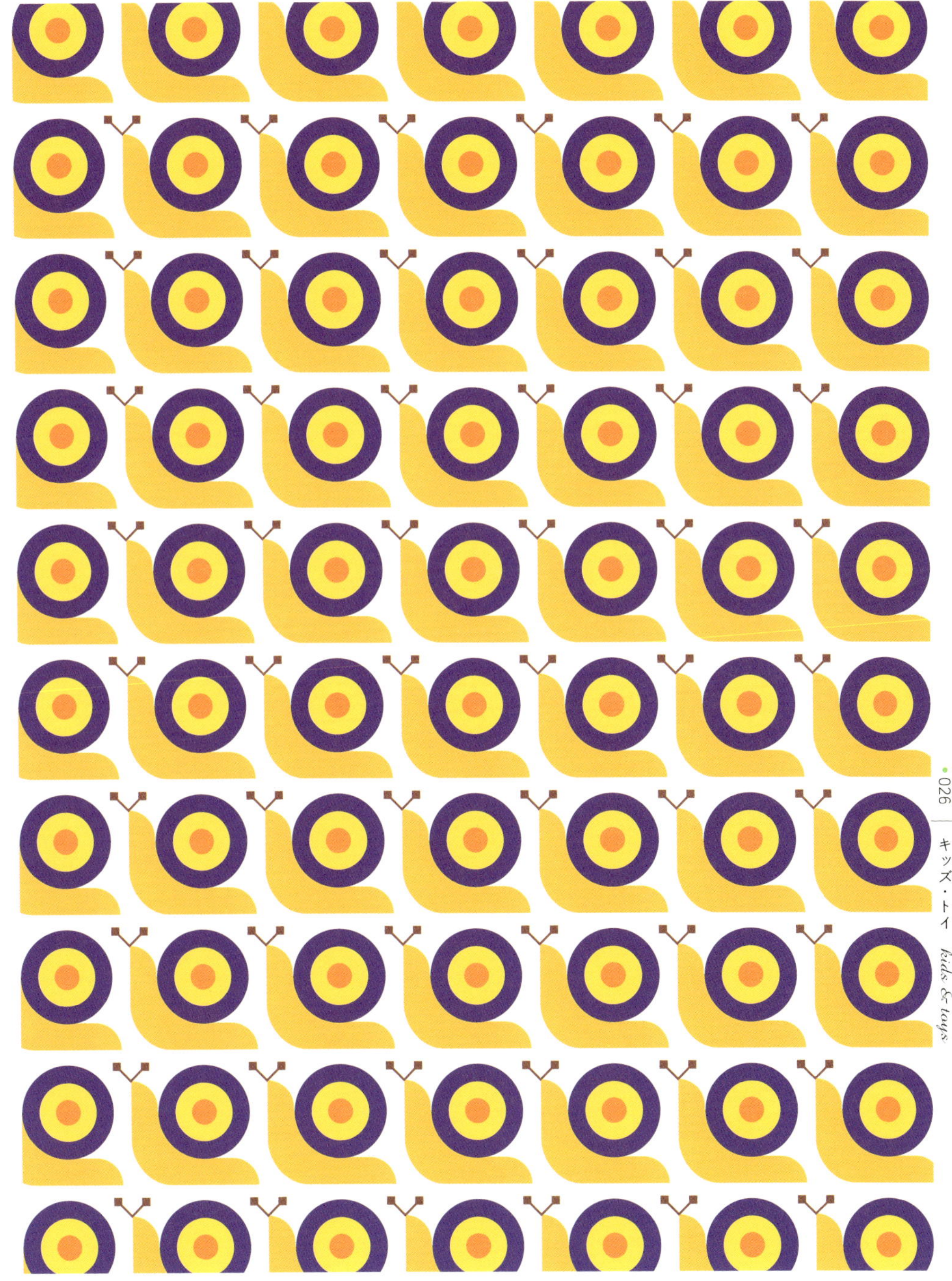

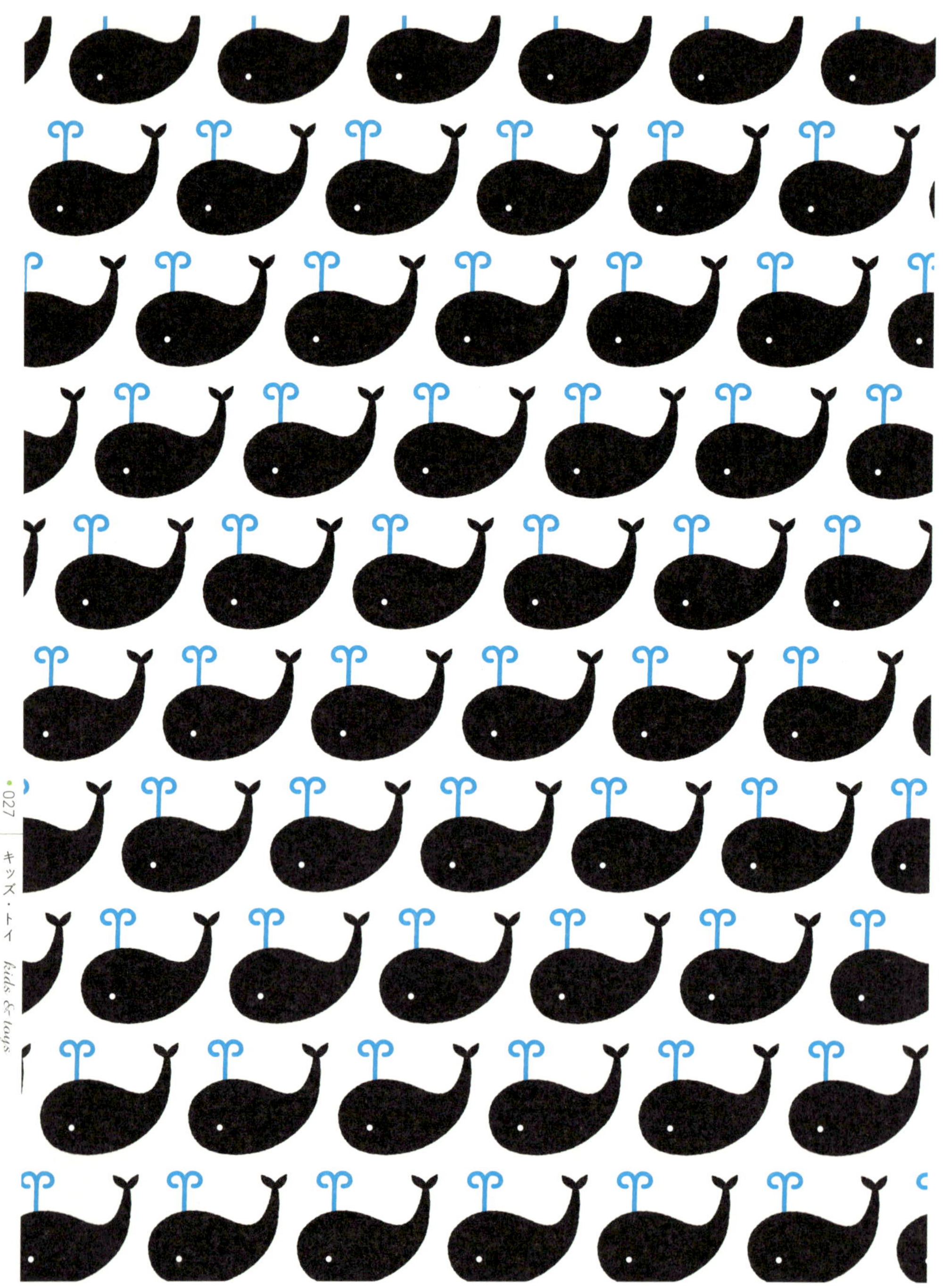

028 キッズ・トイ *kids & toys*

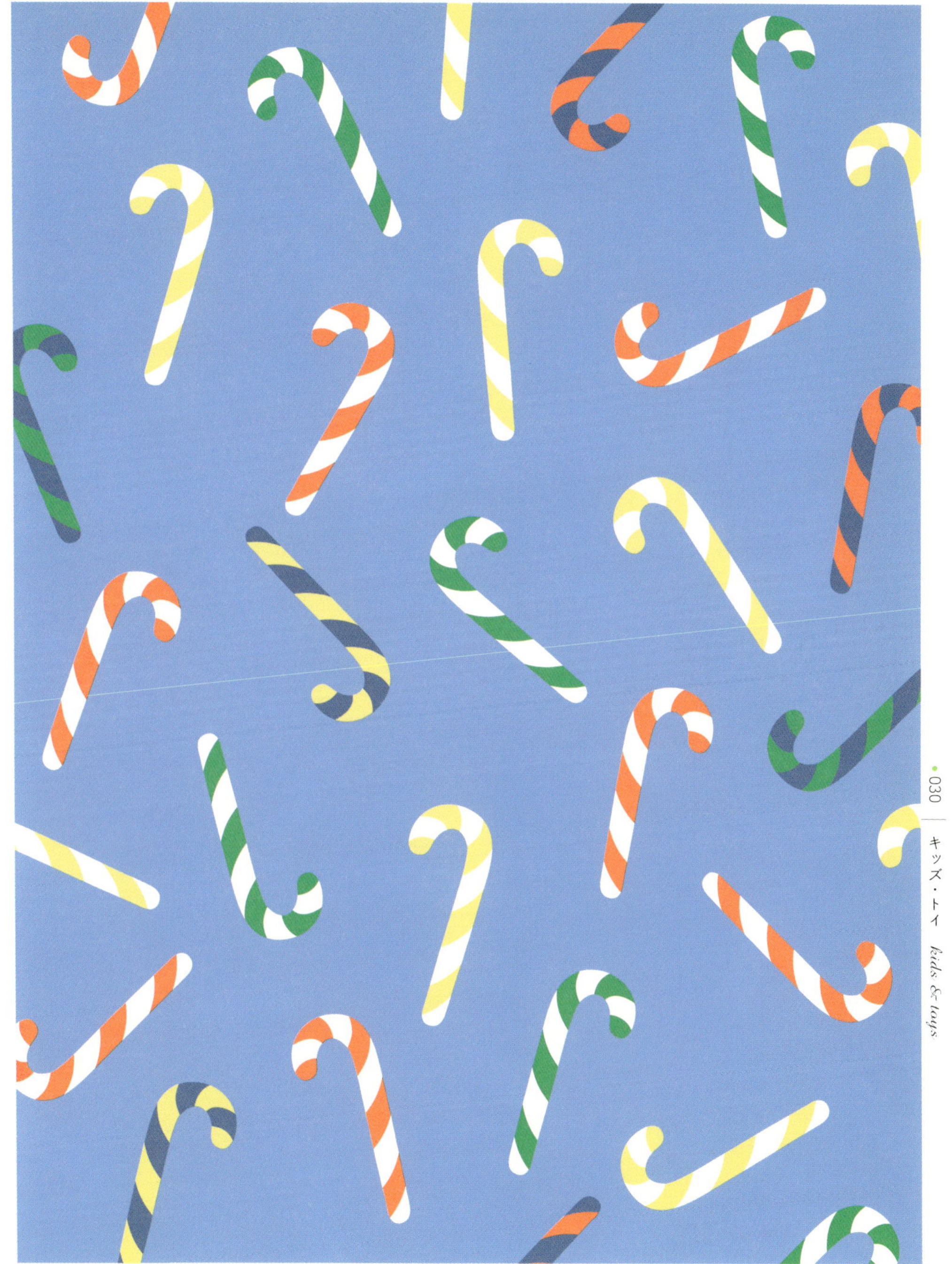

030 キッズ・トイ *kids & toys*

032 キッズ・トイ *kids & toys*

033 キッズ・トイ *kids & toys*

035 キッズ・トイ *kids & toys*

037 キッズ・トイ *kids & toys*

039 キッズ・トイ kids & toys

041 キッズ・トイ *kids & toys*

043 キッズ・トイ *kids & toys*

044

キッズ・トイ *kids & toys*

045

キッズ・トイ *kids & toys*

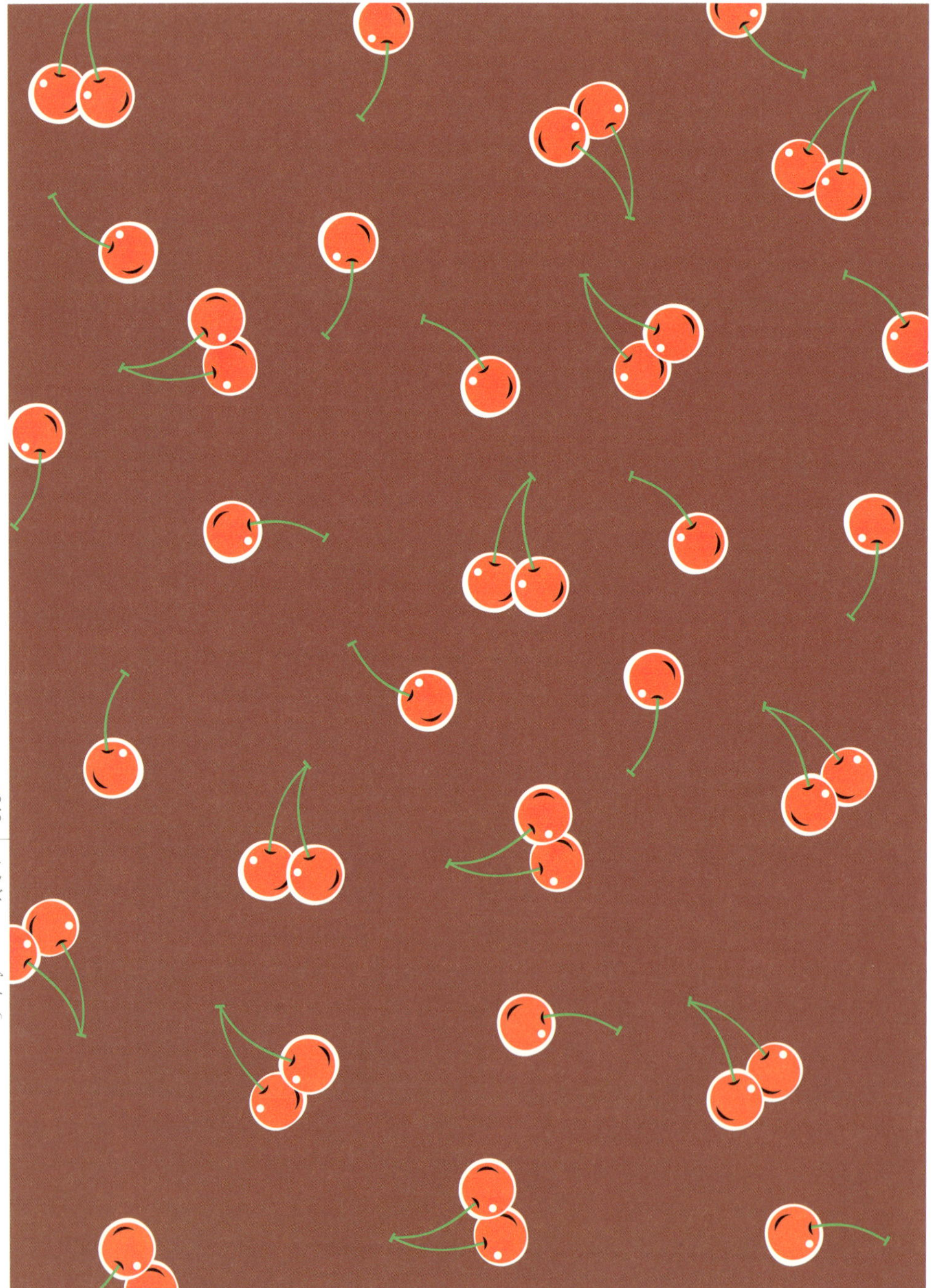

053 キッズ・トイ *kids & toys*

056 キッズ・トイ *kids & toys*

057

●058 | キッズ・トイ *kids & toys*

059 キッズ・トイ *kids & toys*

062 キッズ・トイ *kids & toys*

067

キッズ・トイ *kids & toys*

069 キッズ・トイ *kids & toys*

•071 キッズ・トイ *kids & toys*

072 キッズ・トイ *kids & toys*

077

キッズ・トイ *kids & toys*

078 キッズ・トイ *kids & toys*

080 キッズ・トイ *kids & toys*

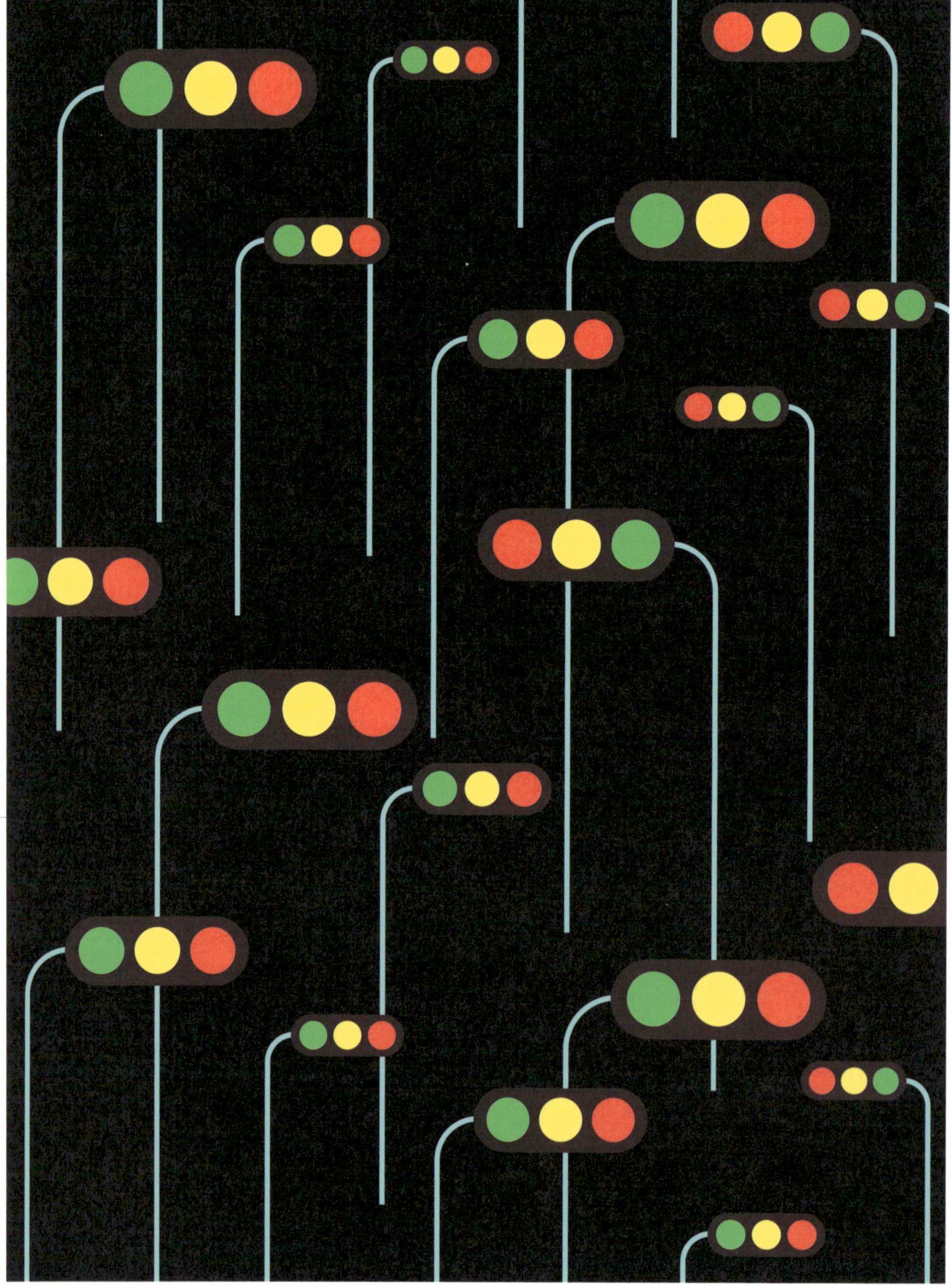

084 キッズ・トイ *kids & toys*

087 キッズ・トイ *kids & toys*

089 キッズ・トイ *kids & toys*

096 | キッズ・トイ kids & toys

097 キッズ・トイ *kids & toys*

098 | キッズ・トイ *kids & toys*

109

キッズ・トイ *kids & toys*

111

キッズ・トイ *kids & toys*

112 キッズ・トイ *kids & toys*

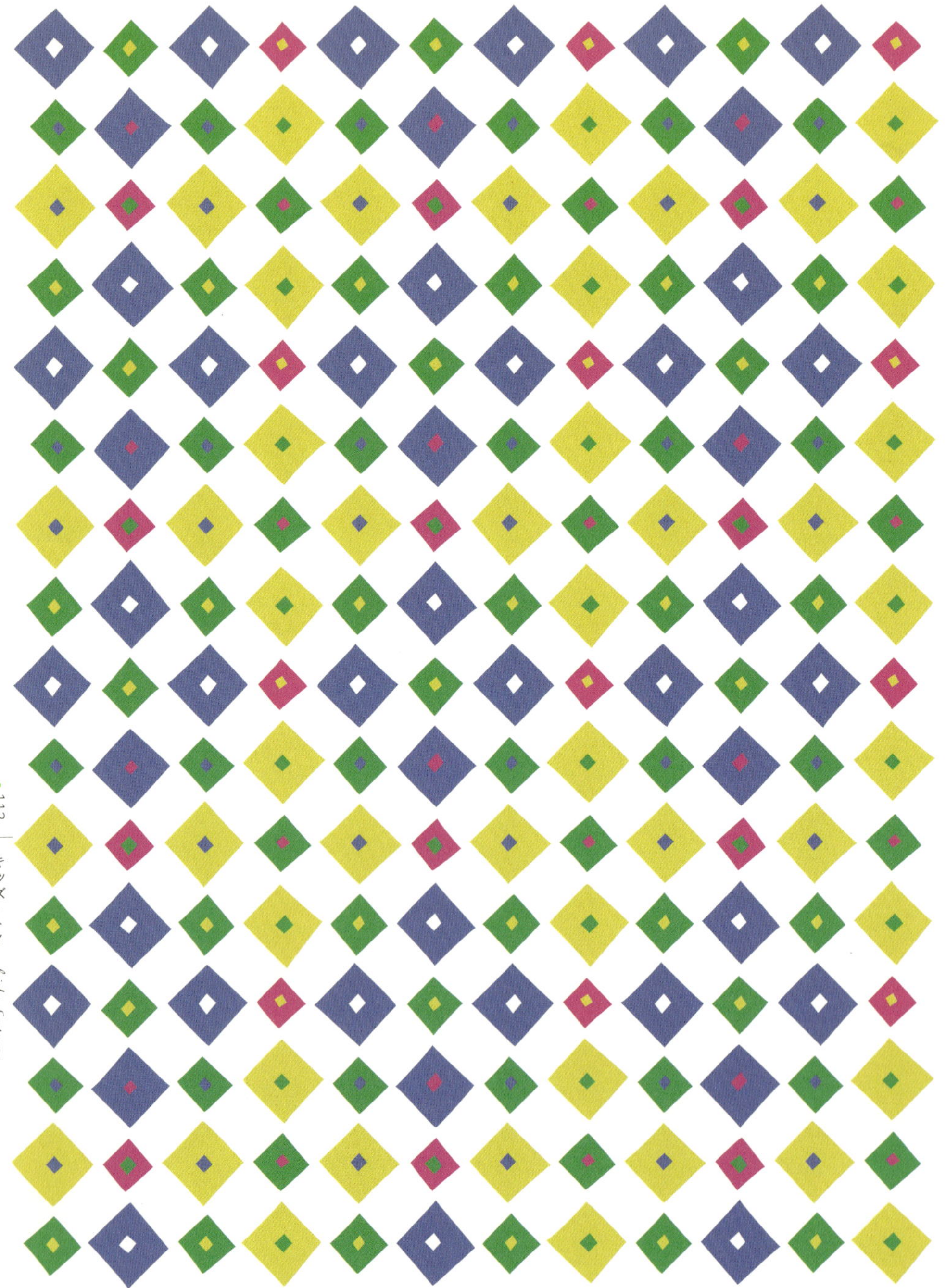

•117 キッズ・トイ *kids & toys*

119 キッズ・トイ *kids & toys*

124 キッズ・トイ *kids & toys*

126 キッズ・トイ *kids & toys*

128 キッズ・トイ *kids & toys*

• 132 | キッズ・トイ *kids & toys*

135

137 キッズ・トイ *kids & toys*

138 キッズ・トイ *kids & toys*

139
キッズ・トイ *kids & toys*

パターンの使い方

(Photoshop & Illustrator)

Petit Pattern Book

how to use patterns

はじめる前に

◯注意すること

- CD-ROMをご使用になる前に、必ずP.175の使用許諾をお読みください。
- 本書では、Mac OS X（10.4.5）、Adobe Photoshop CS2、Adobe Illustrator CS2を用いて解説しています。Windows XP Professional SP1でも動作確認済みですが、環境が異なる場合や、操作方法が分からないときは、OSやソフトウェアに則した、お手持ちの説明書をお読みください。
- 「パターンをつかってつくるもの」（P.164-169）では、Illustratorとプリンタを使用します。

◯準備

まずはCD-ROMをセットして、「Kids-Toys」フォルダを開きます。必要なデータをピックアップしてデスクトップにコピーしましょう。
「Kids-Toys」フォルダを開くと、「JPEG」と「EPS」と「Template」という3つのフォルダが入っています。「Template」フォルダに入っているデータは、P.164以降で使うサンプルデータです。

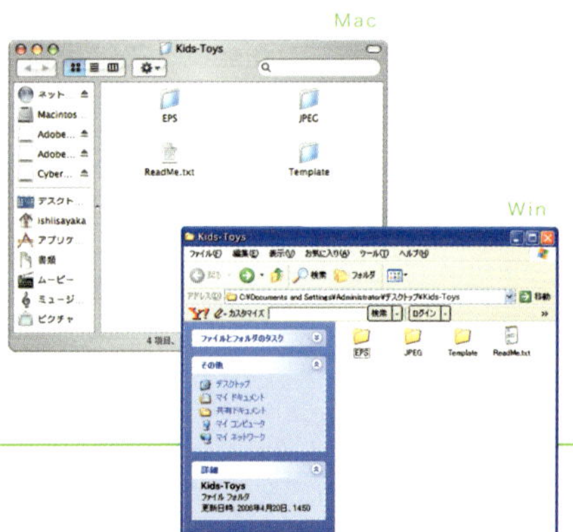

◯データの種類

掲載したすべてのパターンには、それぞれJPEGとEPSの2つの形式でファイルを用意しています。
（EPSファイルは、Illustratorのバージョン8.0で保存しています）

JPEG

＊JPEGファイルとして収録したのは、350dpi（商業印刷に耐え得る解像度）に設定したときに、ほぼA5サイズの印刷面積を持つビットマップ画像。「Adobe Photoshop」をはじめとするビットマップ系のソフトウェアで編集できるほか、多くのソフトウェアで扱うことが可能です。

EPS

＊EPSファイルとして収録したのは、拡大縮小を行っても画質が劣化しない、ベクトル画像。ドロー系のソフトウェア「Adobe Illustrator」でファイルを開くと、自在にカスタマイズできます（ビットマップ系のソフトウェア「Adobe Photoshop」で開くと、「ラスタライズ」という工程を経て、ビットマップイメージに展開します）。

パターンで塗る

tiling

収録したファイルは、どれもタイリング(タイルのように敷き詰めること)が可能な、パターン(繰り返し模様)になっています。Photoshop やIllustratorといったグラフィックソフトウェアで、パターンを登録する機能を使うと、繰り返し模様を一瞬にして好きなだけ、タイリングできます。いずれのソフトウェアでも「塗り」の設定を用いることから、本書ではこれを「パターンで塗る」と呼びます。

パターンで塗るのは初めて、という人に向けて、ここではPhotoshopとIllustratorを用いて、その設定方法を中心に説明していきます。

○データを開く

Photoshop

「ファイル」メニューから「開く」を選択し、パターンファイル(ここではJPEGファイル)を開きます。

Illustrator

「ファイル」メニューから「開く」を選択し、パターンファイル(ここではEPSファイル)を開きます。選んだパターンがページ中央に表れます。

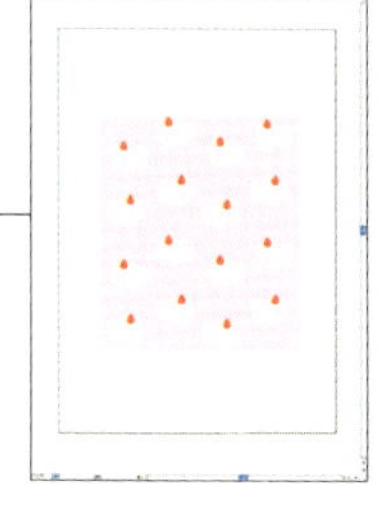

パターンで塗る
tiling

「Photoshop」編

1. パターンを登録する

好きなパターンファイルを選んでPhotoshopで開きます。「選択範囲」メニューから「すべてを選択」を選んでパターン全体を選択し、「編集」メニューから「パターン定義」を選びます。パターンをいつでも使えるように、分かりやすい名前をつけておきます。

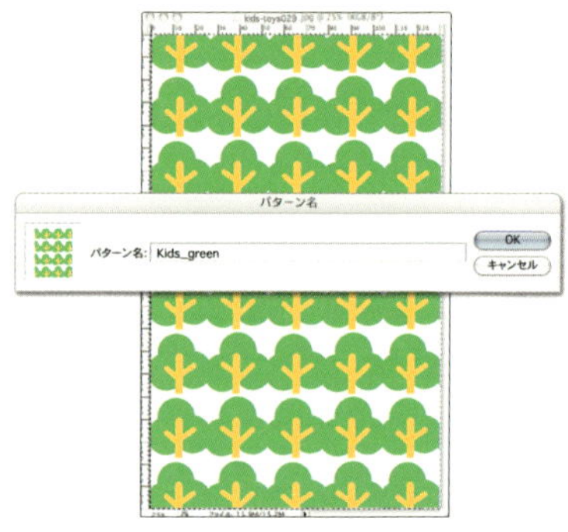

2. 登録したパターンを選ぶ

「ファイル」メニューから「新規」を選んで、パターンで塗りたい空白の画像ファイルを作成します。ツールバーの塗りつぶしツールをダブルクリックし、オプションで「パターン」を選ぶと、先ほど定義したパターンが選択できるようになります。

3. パターンで塗る

塗りつぶしツールで画像上の適当な箇所をクリックして、パターンで塗りつぶします。

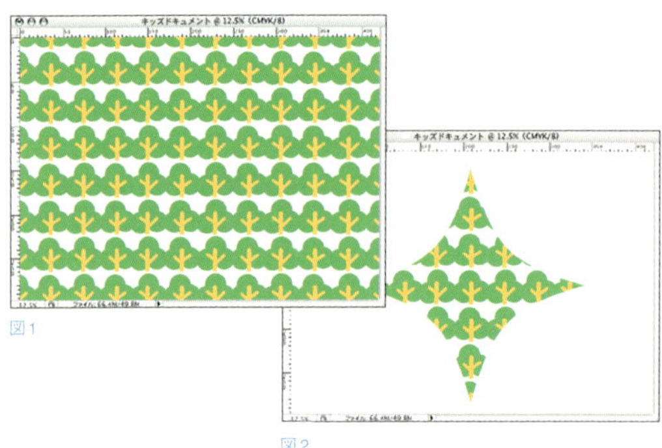

図1

図2

＊図1は、A3サイズの空白のファイルを塗りつぶしたものです。図2のようにあらかじめ選択ツールで塗りつぶす範囲や形を選択しておくと、パターンで選択範囲内のみを塗りつぶすことができます。

パターンで塗る
tiling
「Illustrator」編

1. パターンを登録する

好きなパターンファイルを選んでIllustratorで開きます。「選択」メニューから「すべてを選択」でパターン全体を選択し、「編集」メニューから「コピー」を選ぶとパターンがコピーされます。

「ファイル」メニューから「新規」で空白のドキュメントを作成し、「編集」メニューから「ペースト」を選んでパターンをペーストします。パターン全体が選択された状態のまま、「編集」→「パターン設定」を選んで新規スウォッチを作成し、パターンをいつでも使えるように、分かりやすい名前をつけておきます。

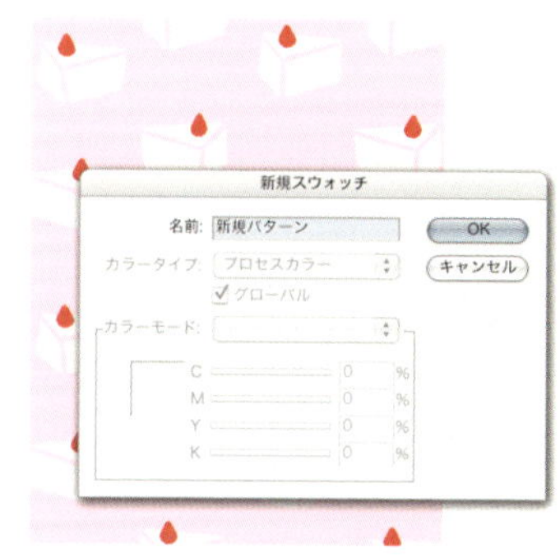

2. 登録したパターンを選ぶ

登録が終わったら、ペーストしたパターンが必要なくなるので、パターン全体が選択された状態のまま、「編集」メニューから「消去」を選んで消します。

「ウインドウ」メニューから「スウォッチ」を選び、スウォッチパレットを表示します。スウォッチパレット内に新たに作成したパターンスウォッチが登録されているので、クリックします。

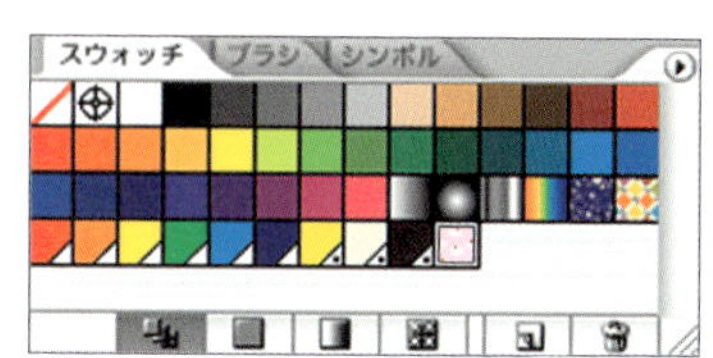

3. パターンで塗る

パターンで塗るオブジェクトを作成します。

図1

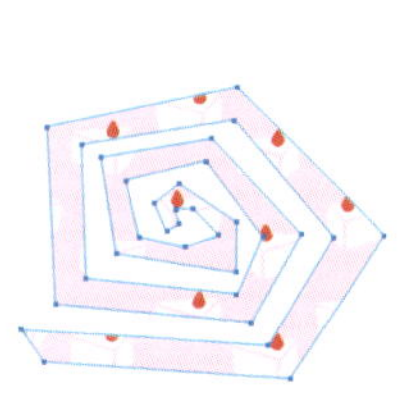
図2

＊図1は、長方形ツールで四角形を描いたものです。図2のように他のドローツールで、パターンで塗りつぶされた複雑なオブジェクトを描くこともできます。

番外編 1

「Illustrator」をつかってパターンの色を変える

Step ❶

IllustratorでEPSファイルを開き、「ウインドウ」メニューから「スウォッチ」を選択して、スウォッチパレットを表示します。続いて、変更したい色のスウォッチをダブルクリックして、「スウォッチオプション」を表示します。

＊収録されたEPSファイルのほとんどは、色や形ごとにレイヤー分けされています。それぞれのレイヤーの順番を入れ替えたり、非表示にしたり、いろいろなアレンジが可能になっています。

Step ❷

「スウォッチオプション」上にあるカラーパレットでCMYKを好きな色に変更します。その際「プレビュー」にチェックを入れておくと、色がパターンにすぐに反映されるので便利です。色が決定したら「OK」をクリックします。

＊Illustratorで開いたEPSファイルは、サイズを変えたり、形を変えたり、要素を足したり引いたりと、自由自在。でも、加工したパターンをスウォッチに登録して使いたい場合は、タイリングで繋がる部分の四辺のアートワークを、加工で崩してしまわないよう気を付けましょう。

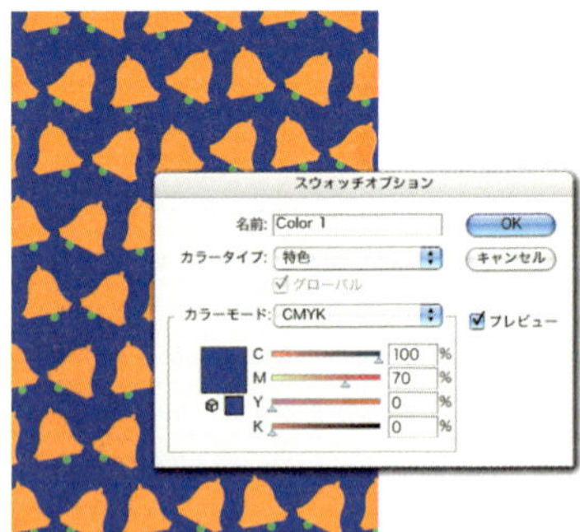

Step ❸

1〜2を繰り返して、オリジナルパターンの出来上がり。別名で保存しておきましょう。

＊Photoshopで開いたJPEGファイルの色を変更することも可能ですが、複雑な輪郭で描かれたパターンは、塗りつぶしツールできれいに色を変更できないことがあります。そういった場合には、「イメージ」メニューから「色調補正」→「カラーバランス」もしくは「色相・彩度」で色味を調整することができます。同じパターンのEPSファイルをまずはIllustratorで開いて色を変更し、別名でJPEG保存したものを、次にPhotoshopで開いて使う方法もあります。

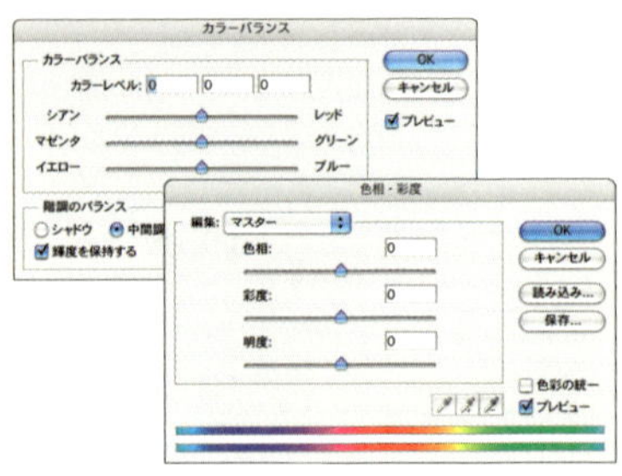

番外編 2

パターンをデスクトップの壁紙にする

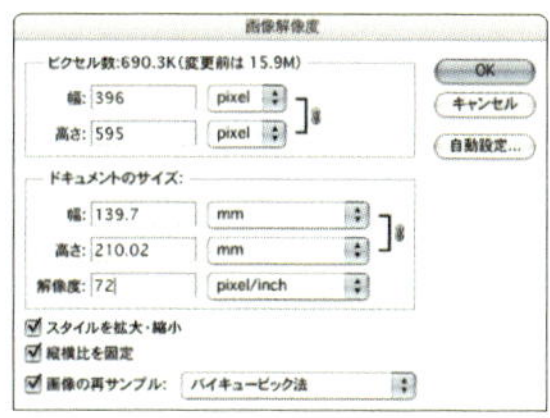

Step ❶

Photoshopで壁紙に設定したいパターンのJPEGファイルを開いて、「イメージ」メニューから「画像解像度」を選択し、モニタ表示に充分な「72dpi」に解像度を設定し直して、別名で保存します。

Step ❷

-for Mac-

Macでは、「アップル」メニューから「システム環境設定」→「デスクトップとスクリーンセーバ」を選択します。「フォルダを選択」から先ほど別名で保存したファイルを指定し、「タイル状に配置」にすると、デスクトップにパターンが表示されます。

-for Windows-

Windowsでは、「コントロールパネル」で「画面」を選択し、「画面のプロパティ」を開きます（デスクトップ上で右クリックして選択することもできます）。「デスクトップ」から先ほど別名で保存したファイルを指定し、「並べて表示」にすると、デスクトップにパターンが表示されます。

and more!

パターンをウェブサイトの背景にする

上のStep ❶で「72dpi」に解像度を設定し直したデータは、ホームページの背景にも使えます。
この際にはJPEGファイルを、写真以外のアートワークの保存に適した、GIF形式に置き換えることをおすすめします。

ブロックパズルをつくる

手のひらサイズのころころしたブロックパズルは、パズルとして組み立てて遊ぶだけでなく、お部屋のインテリアとして飾っておいてもかわいいすぐれものです。

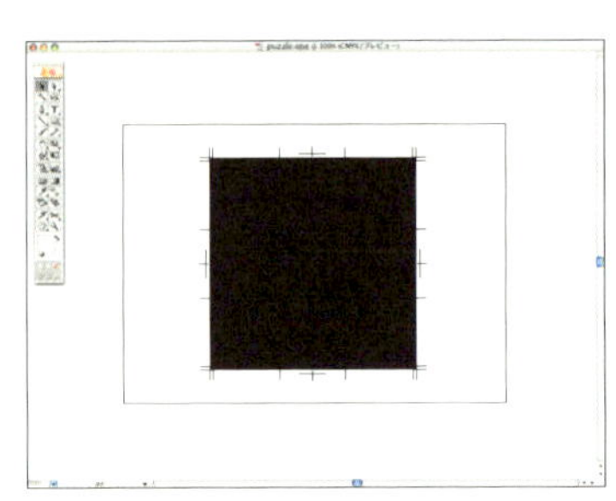

1

○用意するもの

木製ブロック(6cm四方のものを9個)、印刷用紙、定規、カッター、木工用ボンド

1. 台紙データを開く

付属CD-ROMの「Template」フォルダの中にある「puzzle.eps」をデスクトップにコピーし、Illustratorで開きます。

2

2. パターンで塗る

次に、使いたいパターンを「スウォッチ」に登録します(P.161参照)。選択ツールを選び、ドキュメント上のオブジェクトを選択します。選択したオブジェクトの塗りに、先ほど登録したパターンを設定します。

データはブロックの6面分必要なので、それぞれ違うパターンで6種類作り、1種類ずつを別名で保存しておきましょう。ファイルメニューから「別名で保存」を選び、適当なファイル名で保存します。これでデータの出来上がりです。

3

3. プリントする

オブジェクトのサイズは18cm×18cmなので、それがおさまる用紙サイズを選択し、完成した6種類のデータをプリントします。

カット

4

4. カットする

今回CD-ROMに収録した台紙データには、あらかじめトンボ（トリムマーク）がついています。トンボはカットや折り目をつける際に、目印となるものです。

それぞれのパターンを図のようにトンボに合わせてカットします。カットしたパターンがバラバラにならないように気をつけましょう。

5

5.ブロックに貼る

1つのブロックの6面がそれぞれ違うパターンになるように、カットしたパターンを木工用ボンドで丁寧に貼っていきます。

このとき、各ブロックの同じ面に、同じパターンがくるようにしましょう。

出来上がり！

パターンだけでなく、写真やイラストなどを使ってつくっても楽しいですね。

ミニカレンダーをつくる

デスクなどに置くカレンダーは、お気に入りのものを選びたいですね。
パターンを使ったミニカレンダーなら、毎日入れ替えるのが楽しくなります。
万年カレンダーなので、ずっと使うことができます。

1

○用意するもの

MOケース、印刷用紙（フォトマット紙などの工作に適した厚みのある紙）、のり、定規、カッター、鉄筆（なければインクの切れたボールペンや、芯を出さないシャープペンシルなどでも可）

1. 台紙データを開く

付属CD-ROMの「Template」フォルダの中にある「calender.eps」をデスクトップにコピーし、Illustratorで開きます。

データ上にはカレンダーに必要なパーツとして、①パターン台紙、②月（1～12）、③日（十の位、0～3）、④日（一の位、0～9）の4種類があります。

2

2. パターンで塗る

①の6枚のパターン台紙は、左右2つのオブジェクトでできています。それぞれを違うパターンで塗りましょう。

使いたいパターンを12種類、「スウォッチ」に登録します（P.161参照）。選択ツールを選び、ドキュメント上のオブジェクトを選択します。選択したオブジェクトの塗りに、先ほど登録したパターンを設定します。12種類すべて塗り終わったら、データの完成です。

3

3. プリントする

すべてのパーツをプリントします。

4. カットする

今回CD-ROMに収録した台紙データには、あらかじめトンボ（トリムマーク）がついています。トンボはカットや折り目をつける際に、目印となるものです。トンボに合わせてそれぞれのパーツに折りすじを入れ、カットしていきます。

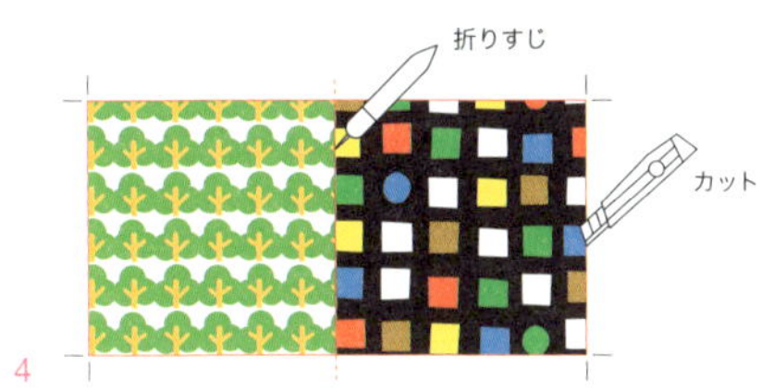

4

5. 貼り合わせる

カットしたパーツを折りすじに合わせて二つ折りにし、裏面をのりで貼り合わせます。

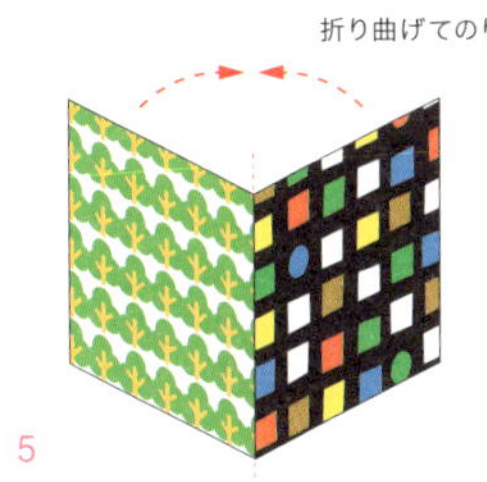

5

6. セットする

①パターン、②月、③日(0〜3)、④日(0〜9)の順で重ね合わせ、図のようにMOケースにセットします。

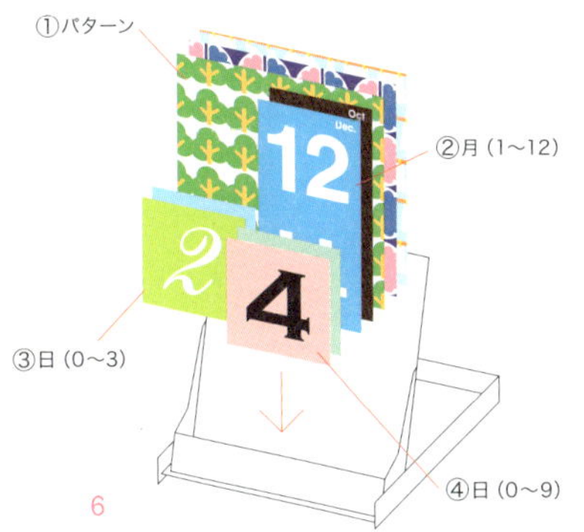

6

出来上がり！

季節や気分にあわせて、背景のパターンを入れ替えてみましょう。使わない時は、ケースを閉じて収納できます。

ペンケースをつくる

どこかなつかしい形のペンケース。毎日使うものだからこそ、
お気に入りのパターンでつくってみましょう。
アイライナーなど、長さのあるコスメを入れてもよいですね。

○用意するもの

専用布用紙、リボン、ボタン、ミシン(なければ手縫いでも可)、手芸用ボンド、はさみ、カッター

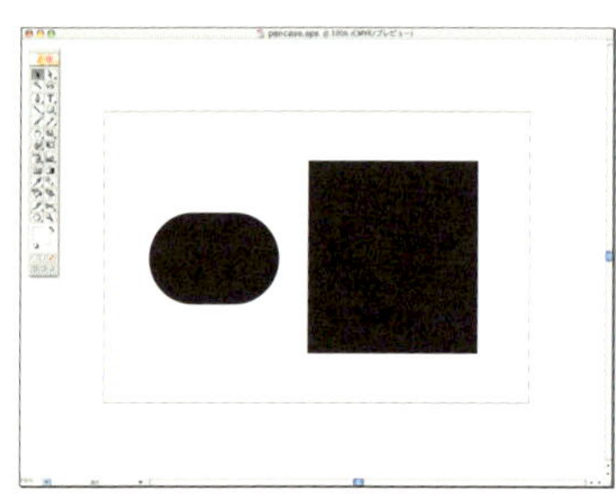

1

1. 台紙データを開く

付属CD-ROMの「Template」フォルダの中にある「pencase.eps」をデスクトップにコピーし、Illustratorで開きます。データ上にはふたと本体の2種類のパーツがあります。

ふた

本体

2

2. パターンで塗る

ふたの表裏や色の組み合わせを考えながら、使いたいパターンを「スウォッチ」に登録します(P.161参照)。選択ツールを選び、ドキュメント上のオブジェクトを選択します。選択したオブジェクトの塗りに、先ほど登録したパターンを設定します。これでデータの出来上がりです。

3

3. 専用布用紙にプリントしてカットする

プリンタに専用布用紙をセットしてプリントします。今回使用している用紙は裏面にPETフィルムが貼られたタイプのものですが、同じように用紙には表裏があるので注意してセットしましょう(プリントの際の細かな設定は、各製品に記載されている注意事項に従って設定してください)。プリントが終わったら、周りの不要な部分をカットし、裏に貼られているPETフィルムをはがします。

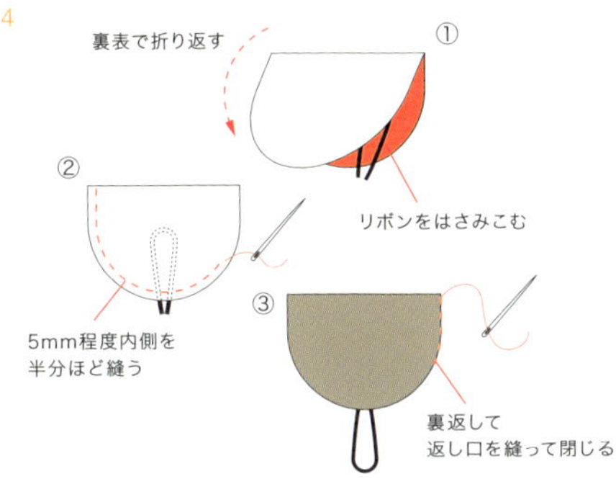

4. ふたを縫製する

まず、ふたを縫製します。①ふたの部分を裏返して半分に折ります。②ふたの中心にリボンをはさみ、端から5mm程度内側を半分ほど縫い合わせます。③開いている返し口から裏返し、縫って閉じます。

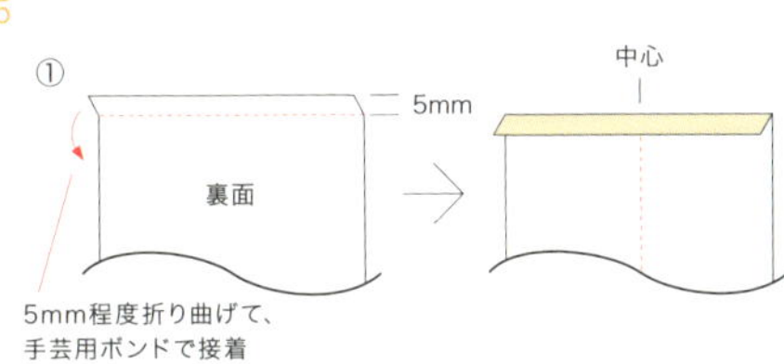

5. 本体にふたを縫いつける

次に、本体にふたを縫いつけます。①本体の上部を5mm程度折り曲げ、手芸用ボンドで接着します。ボンドが乾いたら本体をいったん二つ折りにして、折りあとを残して中心が分かるようにしておきます。②つづいて、図のように本体のパターンが印刷されている面の中心にふたの端を合わせて、縫いしろを5mm程度取ってふたを縫いつけます。③本体を折り返し、L字型に縫い合わせます。

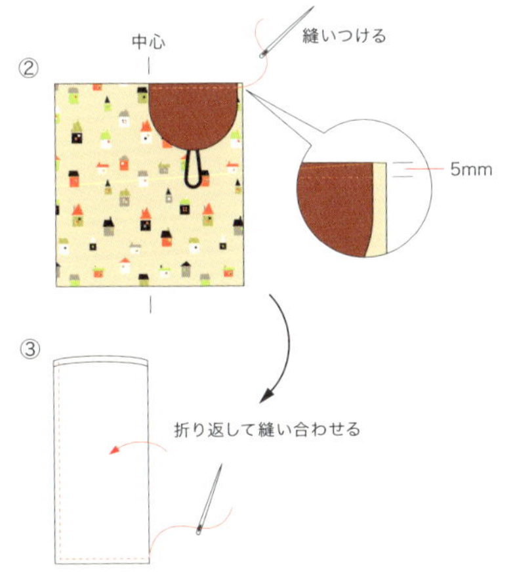

6. ボタンをとりつける

縫い終わったら本体を裏返し、リボンのかかる位置にボタンをとりつけます。ふたを閉じてみて、ちょうど良い位置を確認しながらとりつけましょう。

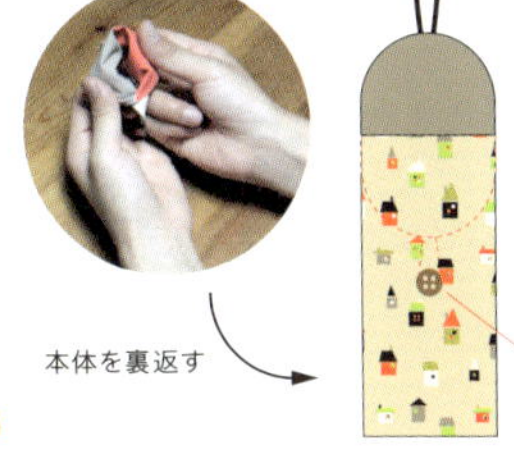

出来上がり！

キッズ・トイ
kids & toys

おしゃれなパターン素材集
Petit Pattern Book

001
kids-toys001

002
kids-toys002

003
kids-toys003

004
kids-toys004

005
kids-toys005

006
kids-toys006

007
kids-toys007

008
kids-toys008

009
kids-toys009

010
kids-toys010

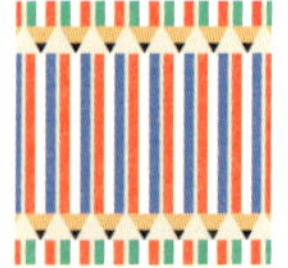
011
kids-toys011

012
kids-toys012

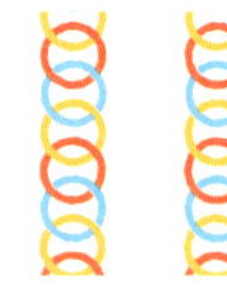
013
kids-toys013

014
kids-toys014

015
kids-toys015

016
kids-toys016

017
kids-toys017

018
kids-toys018

019
kids-toys019

020
kids-toys020

021
kids-toys021

022
kids-toys022

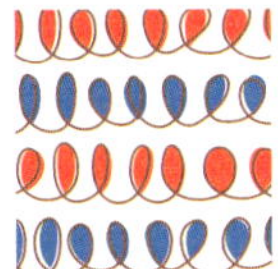
023
kids-toys023

024
kids-toys024

025
kids-toys025

026
kids-toys026

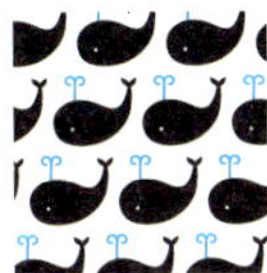
027
kids-toys027

028
kids-toys028

029
kids-toys029

030
kids-toys030

031
kids-toys031

032
kids-toys032

033
kids-toys033

034
kids-toys034

035
kids-toys035

036
kids-toys036

037
kids-toys037

038
kids-toys038

039
kids-toys039

040
kids-toys040

041
kids-toys041

042
kids-toys042

043
kids-toys043

044
kids-toys044

045
kids-toys045

046
kids-toys046

047
kids-toys047

048
kids-toys048

049
kids-toys049

050
kids-toys050

051
kids-toys051

052
kids-toys052

053
kids-toys053

054
kids-toys054

055
kids-toys055

056
kids-toys056

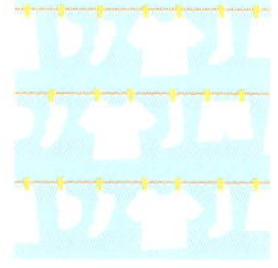
057
kids-toys057

058
kids-toys058

059
kids-toys059

060
kids-toys060

061
kids-toys061

062
kids-toys062

063
kids-toys063

064
kids-toys064

065
kids-toys065

066
kids-toys066

067
kids-toys067

068
kids-toys068

069
kids-toys069

070
kids-toys070

071
kids-toys071

072
kids-toys072

073
kids-toys073

074
kids-toys074

075
kids-toys075

076
kids-toys076

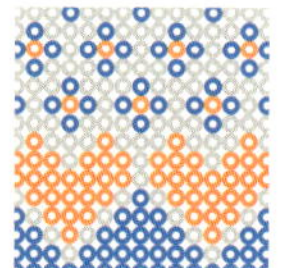
077
kids-toys077

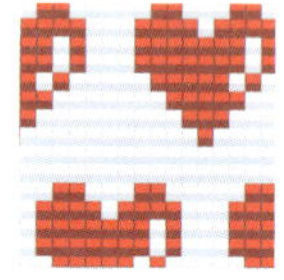
078
kids-toys078

079
kids-toys079

080
kids-toys080

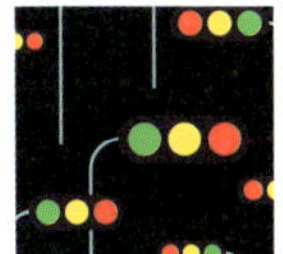
081
kids-toys081

082
kids-toys082

083
kids-toys083

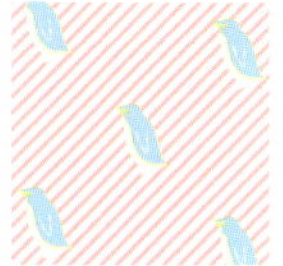
084
kids-toys084

085
kids-toys085

086
kids-toys086

087
kids-toys087

088
kids-toys088

089
kids-toys089

090
kids-toys090

091
kids-toys091

092
kids-toys092

093
kids-toys093

094
kids-toys094

095
kids-toys095

096
kids-toys096

097
kids-toys097

098
kids-toys098

099
kids-toys099

100
kids-toys100

101
kids-toys101

102
kids-toys102

103
kids-toys103

104
kids-toys104

105
kids-toys105

106
kids-toys106

107
kids-toys107

108
kids-toys108

109
kids-toys109

110
kids-toys110

111
kids-toys111

112
kids-toys112

113
kids-toys113

114
kids-toys114

115
kids-toys115

116
kids-toys116

117
kids-toys117

118
kids-toys118

119
kids-toys119

120
kids-toys120

121
kids-toys121

122
kids-toys122

123
kids-toys123

124
kids-toys124

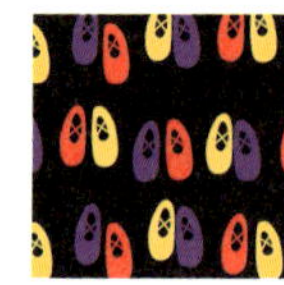
125
kids-toys125

126
kids-toys126

127
kids-toys127

128
kids-toys128

129
kids-toys129

130
kids-toys130

131
kids-toys131

132
kids-toys132

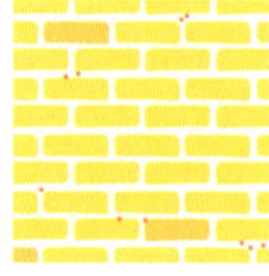
133
kids-toys133

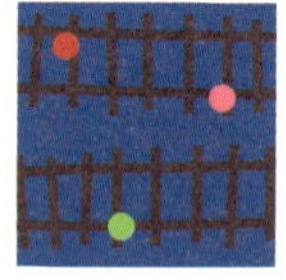
134
kids-toys134

135
kids-toys135

136
kids-toys136

137
kids-toys137

138
kids-toys138

139
kids-toys139

140
kids-toys140

『おしゃれなパターン素材集　キッズ・トイ』
付属CD-ROM使用許諾書（ソフトウェアライセンス契約書）

1. ライセンス

1）株式会社ビー・エヌ・エヌ新社（以下「弊社」という。）は、本製品を購入され、本使用許諾書記載の条件に合意されたお客様（以下「ユーザー」という。）に対し、本ソフトウェアを同時に1台のコンピュータ上でのみ使用できる、譲渡不能の非独占的権利を許諾します。

2）ユーザーは、2の「制限事由」に該当する場合を除き、本ソフトウェアに含まれる素材を加工・編集し、もしくは他の素材と組み合わせるなどして、主に以下のデザインに使用することができます。

○WEBなどのデジタルメディア

○店舗の内装、案内表示、レジにおける無料パッケージなどのグラフィックツール

○印刷物として頒布するチラシ、フライヤー、ポスター、DM、カタログ、パンフレットなどの広告・販売促進ツール

○個人制作・個人利用の雑貨、服、グリーティングカード、名刺など

（個人的・職業的・商業的用途の利用を認めますが、いずれも非売品のデザインに限ります。個人においても素材を利用した制作物の販売は行えません。次の制限事由をよくお読み下さい。）

2. 制限事由

以下の行為を禁止します。

1）本ソフトウェアを1台のコンピュータで使用するためのやむを得ぬ場合を除き、本ソフトウェアを複製すること

2）本使用許諾書に基づくライセンスを他に譲渡し、本製品の貸与もしくはその他の方法て本ソフトウェアを他者に使用させること

3）流通を目的とした商品のデザインに素材を利用すること（書籍や雑誌など、有料の印刷物を含む。）

4）商品パッケージおよび有料のギフトパッケージに素材を利用すること

5）素材をブランドイメージとして利用すること（可能性があると判断できるものも含む。）

6）素材を利用してポストカード、名刺、雑貨などの制作販売または制作サービスを行うこと

7）素材を利用してインターネットによるダウンロードサービスを行うこと（グリーティングカード・サービスを含む。）

8）素材をホームページ上で公開する場合に、オリジナルデータがダウンロード可能となる環境を作ること

9）ソフトウェア製品等を製造・販売するために素材を流用すること

10）素材そのものや素材を用いた制作物について意匠権などの権利を取得すること

11）素材を公序良俗に反する目的、誹謗・中傷目的で利用すること

※本素材を使用した商業デザインや商品販売等をお考えの際にはご相談に応じます。

事前に下記までご連絡ください。

○有限会社二メートル〇九センチグラフィックス（fax：03-3470-2356　e-mail：info@209g.com）

3. 著作権、その他の知的財産権

本ソフトウェアおよび素材に関する著作権、その他の知的財産権は、弊社または弊社への供給者の排他的財産として留保されています。素材を利用した制作物においてユーザーの著作権を明示する場合は、併せてパターンの著作権「©2007 2m09cmGRAPHICS, Inc.」を明示してください。

4. 責任の制限

弊社および弊社への供給者は、請求原因の如何を問わず、本ソフトウェアの使用または使用の不能および素材の利用から生じるすべての損害や不利益（利益の逸失およびデータの損壊を含む。）につき、一切責任を負わないものとします。

5. 使用許諾の終了

ユーザーが本使用許諾書に違反した場合、弊社は、本使用許諾書に基づくユーザーのライセンスを終了させることができます。

Petit Pattern Book

How to use patterns

(Photoshop & Illustrator)

Before you start

○ Notes

- Please read the License Agreement on page 190 before you start.
- The explanation in this book is based on Mac OS X (10.4.5), Adobe Photoshop CS2, and Adobe Illustrator CS2. The functionality has also been verified with Windows XP Professional SP1. If your system is different, or if you have a question concerning the operation of the software, refer to the manuals corresponding to your OS and software.
- In the chapter "Let's use the patterns to make an original article" (p184-189), you will be using Illustrator and your printer.

○ Preparation

At first, set the attached CD-ROM and open "Kids-Toys" folder. Pick up the patterns you need and copy them to your desktop.

Open the folder "Kids-Toys" and you will find three folders: "JPEG", "EPS", and "Template". You are going to use the data inside "Template" from p184 as sample data later on.

Mac

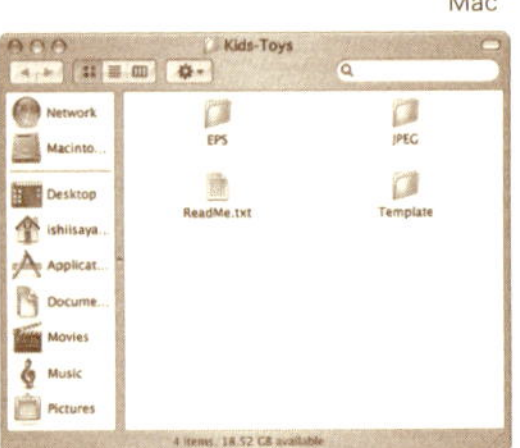

○ Different kinds of data

All the patterns in the book are prepared in the following two formats:
(EPS files are saved with Illustrator 8.0.)

JPEG

※In the JPEG file, you will find bitmap images which are printed on the surface of around 148× 210mm at 350 dpi (the resolution suitable for commercial printing). You can edit them with Adobe Photoshop and other bitmap software, and you can use it with many other types of software.

EPS

※In the EPS file, you will find vector images, which do not deteriorate when you increase or reduce the size. Open the file with Adobe Illustrator or other drawing software, and you will be able to customize the images freely (When you open the file with bitmap software such as Adobe Photoshop, the image will be developed as a bitmap image after the process called rasterizing).

Tiling with a pattern

All the files are repeated patterns which can be tiled. Register patterns in Photoshop, Illustrator or other graphic software, and you can tile one of the repeated patterns in the blink of an eye.

For those people who have never tiled with patterns, we shall explain how to do it using Photoshop and Illustrator, focusing on the settings.

● Open the data

Photoshop

Select "Open" from the "File" menu, and open the pattern file (JPEG file here).

Illustrator

Select "Open" from the "File" menu, and open the pattern file (EPS file here). The pattern chosen will appear in the centre of the screen.

How to tile with
Photoshop

1. Save the pattern

Open your favorite pattern with Photoshop. Select the whole image by choosing "Select" → "All", and select "Edit" → "Define Pattern". Give the pattern an easily recognized name so that you can use it whenever you want.

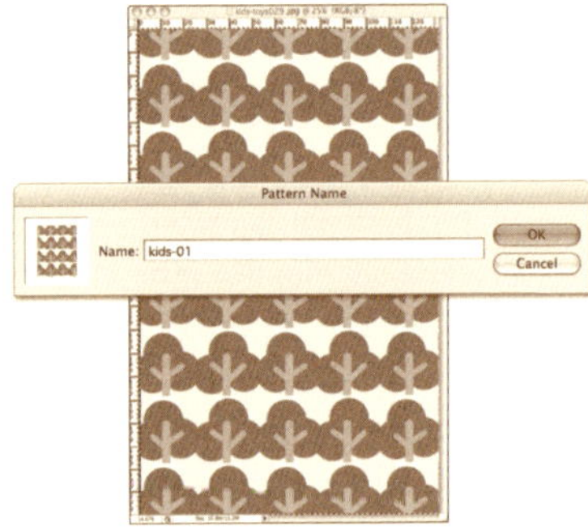

2. Select the saved pattern

Select "File" → "New" and create a blank image file to be filled with the pattern. Double click on Paint Bucket Tool and select "Pattern" from the options, and you are able to choose the pattern you have already defined.

3. Tiling with the pattern

Click on the image with the Paint Bucket Tool and tile the whole image with the pattern.

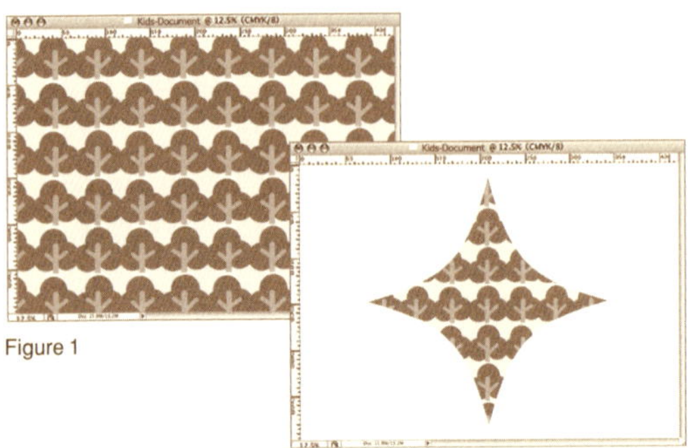

Figure 1

Figure 2

※Figure1 shows a blank 420× 297mm file tiled with a pattern. If you use Select tools to select the part of the image to be tiled, you can tile only the part and the shape you have selected.

How to tile with
Illustrator

1. Save the pattern

Open your favorite pattern with Illustrator. Select the whole image by choosing "Select"→"All", and "Edit"→"Copy" to copy the pattern.

Create a blank document by selecting "File"→"New", and paste the pattern by selecting "Edit"→"Paste". While the whole pattern is still selected, select "Edit"→"Define Pattern" to create a new swatch and give it an easily recognized name so that you can use it whenever you want.

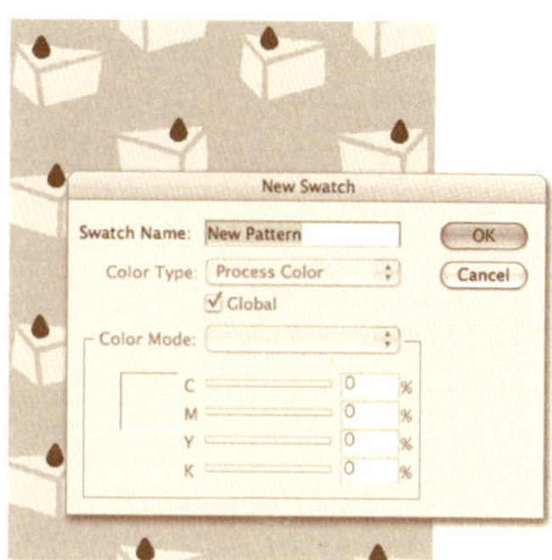

2. Select the saved pattern

When you have saved the image, delete the pattern you pasted previously, as you do not need it any more. While the whole pattern is still selected, select "Edit"→"Clear" and the pattern will be deleted.

Select "Window"→"Swatches" to show the swatch pallet. Click the newly registered pattern on the swatch pallet.

3. Tiling with the pattern

Make an object to be tiled with the pattern.

Figure 1

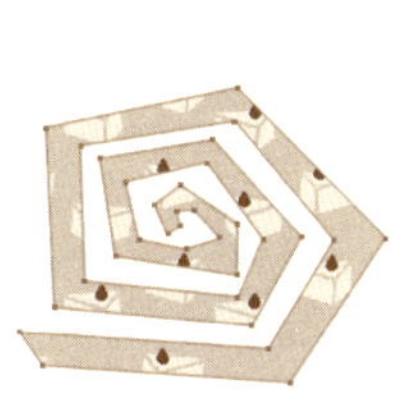

Figure 2

※Figure 1 shows a rectangular shape drawn with the Rectangular Tool. You can also draw a complicated object tiled with the pattern with other tools, as shown in Figure 2.

How to change the color of a pattern with Illustrator

Step 1

Open the EPS file with Illustrator (see p179). Select "Window"→"Swatches" to show the swatch pallet. Double click the swatch of the color you would like to change to show "Swatch Options".

※Most of the EPS files have different layers for each color and shape: you can arrange the patterns by changing the layer orders or hiding a layer.

Step 2

Modify CMYK on the color pallet on "Swatch Options" to create your own color. You can select the "Preview" option beforehand to show the new color immediately. When you have obtained the color you want, click "OK".

※If you have opened the EPS file with Illustrator, you can modify the pattern any way you like: by changing the size, the shape, adding or taking out an element, etc. On the other hand, if you would like to save the modified pattern in Swatch for future use, avoid breaking the square artwork of its four sides, which would be juxtaposed on the tiling image.

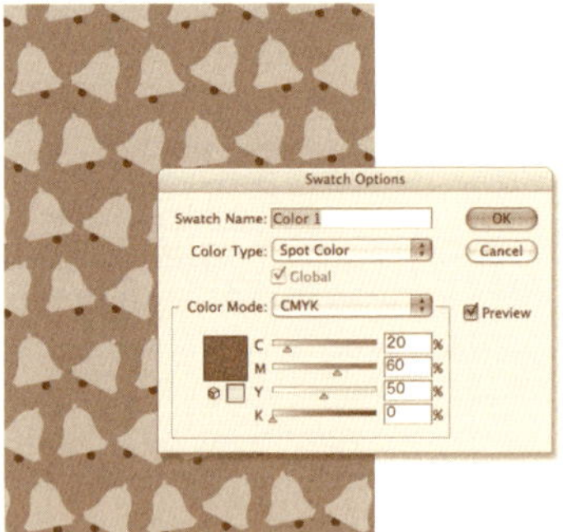

Step 3

Repeat 1-2 and create your own original pattern. Save it under a different name.

※While it is also possible to change the color of the JPEG file with Photoshop using the Paint Bucket Tool, the new color may be fuzzy in some patterns drawn using complicated lines. If this happens, select "Image"→"Adjustments"→"Color Balance" or "Hue/Saturation" to correct the color. Alternatively, open the EPS file of the same pattern with Illustrator, change the color, save as a JPEG file under a different name, and open and use it with Photoshop.

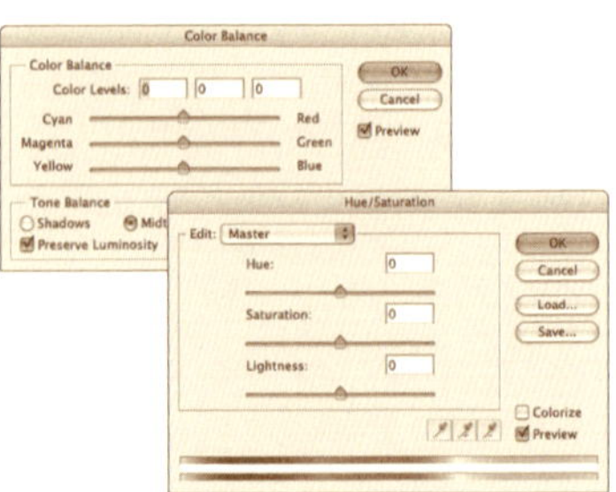

How to use the pattern as a desktop background of your computer

Step 1

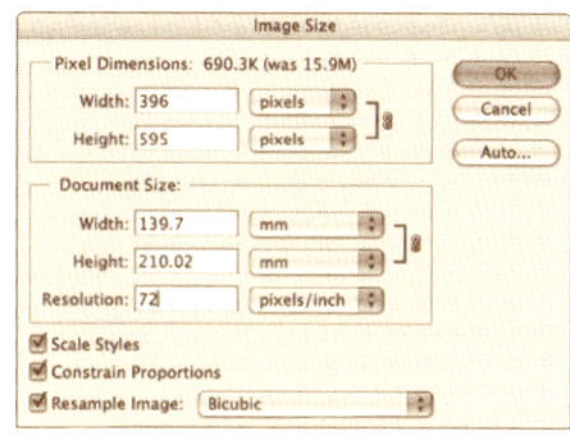

Open the JPEG file with Photoshop (see p179), select "Image"→"Image Size". Change the resolution to "72 dpi", the resolution suitable for the monitor, and save it under a new name.

Step 2

-for Mac-

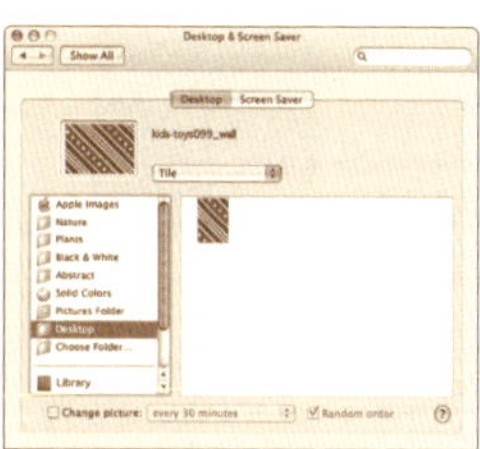

Go to the "Apple" menu and select "System Preferences"→"Desktop & Screen Saver". Select the saved file in Step1 for the desktop background, and choose "Tile" to make the pattern appear on the desktop.

-for Windows-

Go to "Control Panel", and open "Display Properties" (you can also select it by right-clicking your mouse on the desktop). Click the "Desktop" tab, select the saved file in Step1 for the background, and chose "Tile" to show the pattern on the desktop.

Using the pattern for the background of your website

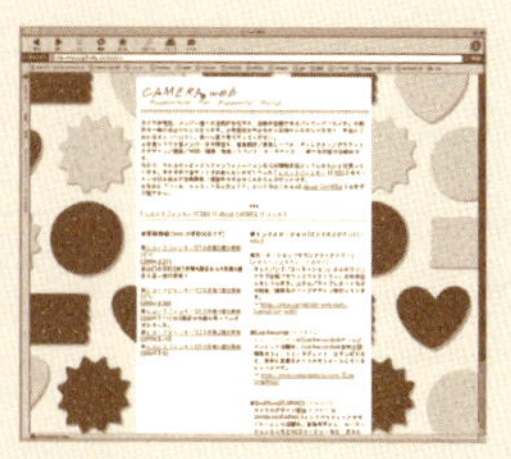

The data at resolution "72 dpi" at Step1 above can also be used as the background of a website.
In this case, it is recommended that you transfer the date to the GIF format, which is suitable for saving artworks other than photos.

How to make a "block puzzle"

Create a beautiful, palm-sized block puzzle. You can have fun playing with the puzzle, but it will also serve as a charming decoration in your home.

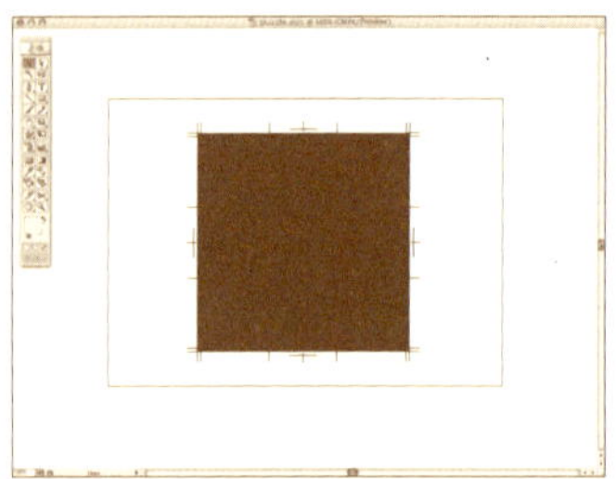

1

○You will need:

9 wooden cubes (6cm each side), printing paper, a ruler, a cutter and glue for wooden surfaces

1. Open the mount data

Find the "puzzle.eps" file in the "Template" folder in the attached CD-ROM. Copy it on to the hard disk, and open it with Illustrator.

Save As
Save: puzzle_01.eps
Format: Illustrator EPS (eps)
Where: Desktop
Use Adobe Dialog
Cancel Save

2

2. Tile with the patterns

Register the pattern you have chosen in "Swatch" (see p.181). Click on the "Select" tool and select the object on the document. Select the pattern which you have saved to paint the selected object.

You need six different sets of data for the six sides of the cubes. Select six different patterns and save them under different names. Click the "File" menu and select "Save As..." to save each pattern. Now the data are ready.

3

3. Printing

Use printing paper large enough for the objects (18cm×18cm) and print out six different sets of data.

4. Cutting

The mount in the CD-ROM is already marked with trimming lines, which serve as guidelines for creasing and cutting.

Cut each pattern out with a cutter along the trimming lines as shown in the figures on the left. Gather all the pieces of printed pattern together to avoid missing any.

Cut

4

5. Glue on the cubes

Carefully glue a piece of each pattern on to each cube, so that each cube has six different faces.

Take care to glue each piece of the patterns on to the correct side of the cubes.

5

Now the puzzle is ready!

Try using pictures and drawings instead of the patterns.

How to make a "mini calender"

Create your own mini calender for your desktop.
It's a fun to change the day card every day
if it is made using a pattern you have chosen.
You can use this calender over and over.

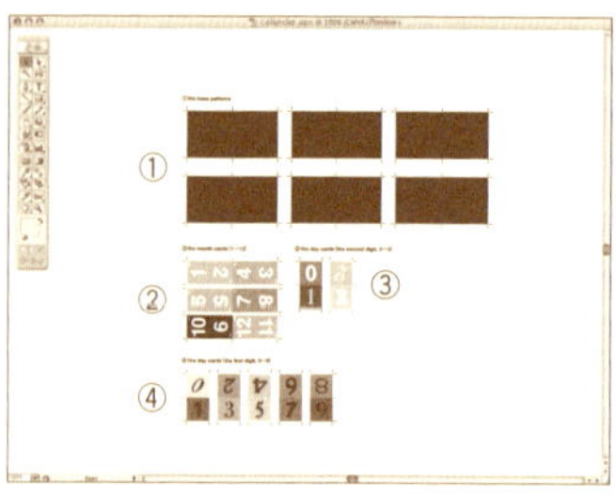

1

○You will need:

A MO disc case, printing paper (such as photo-mat paper - the paper you use should be strong enough for artwork), glue, a ruler, a cutter, and a tracer (You can also use a ballpoint pen that has run out of ink or a propelling pencil with no lead)

1. Open the mount data

Find the "calender.eps" file in the "Template" folder in the attached CD-ROM. Copy it on to the hard disk, and open it with Illustrator.

In the mount, you'll find four objects which are necessary parts of the calender: ① the base patterns, ② the month cards (1-12), ③ the day cards (the second digit, 0-3) and ④ the day cards (the first digit, 0-9)

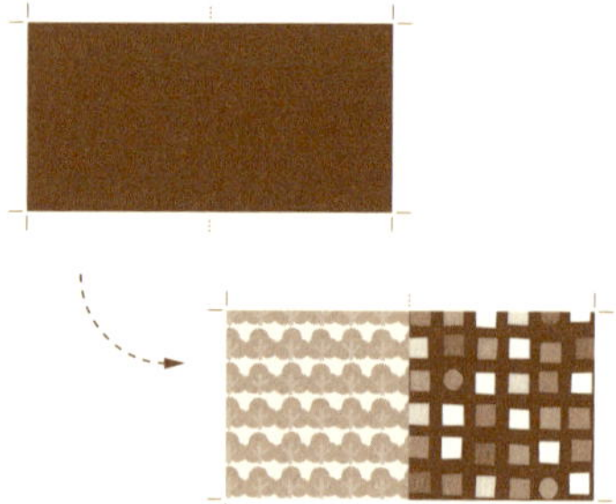
2

2. Tile with the pattern

The six base patterns ① are divided equally into two squares. Tile the squares with different patterns.

Register the twelve different patterns you have chosen in "Swatch" (see p.181). Click on the "Select" tool and select the object on the document. Select the patterns which you have saved to paint the selected object. Once you have tiled all twelve objects, the data are ready to use.

3

3. Printing

Print out all the parts.

4. Cutting

The mount in the CD-ROM is already marked with trimming lines, which serve as guidelines for creasing and cutting. Crease along the trimming lines and cut out all the parts.

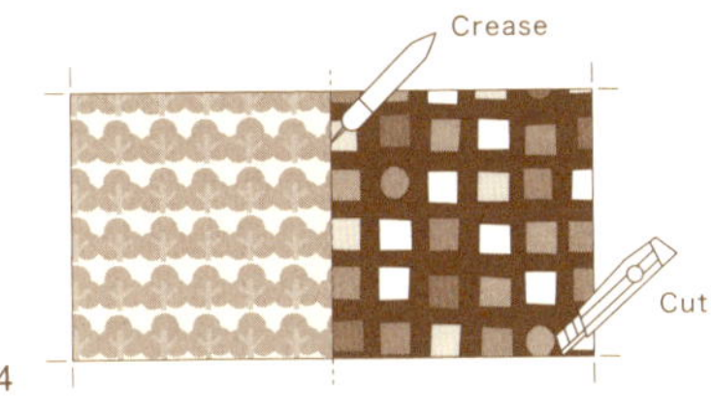

4

5. Gluing

With the non-printed side inside, fold the base patterns in two along the crease and glue them together.

Fold in two and glue together

5

6. Setting

Insert, firstly ①the base pattern, secondly ②the month cards, then ③the day cards (0-3) and finally ④the day cards (0-9) into the MO case as shown in the figures on the left.

Now the calender is ready!

Change the base pattern according to the season and your fancy. You can close the casebox and put it away whenever you don't need it.

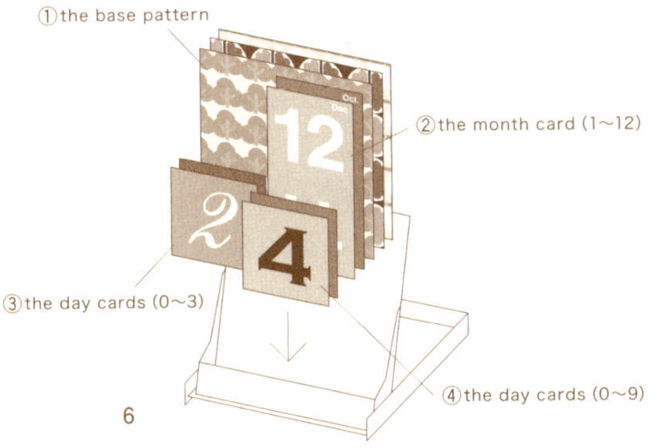

6

How to make a "pencase"

This pencase might bring back memories of your childhood. Choose the pattern you like best to make this pencase, as you will use it everyday. You can also put an eyeliner or other long toilet articles in this case.

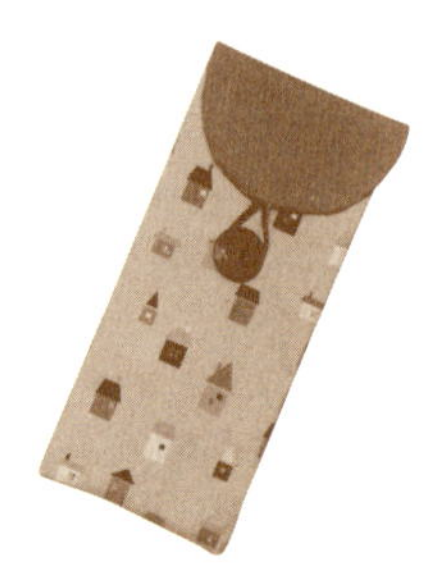

○You will need:

Canvas cloth made for use with a printer, ribbon, a button, a sewing machine (optional as you can sew by hand), glue for the cloth, a pair of scissors and a cutter

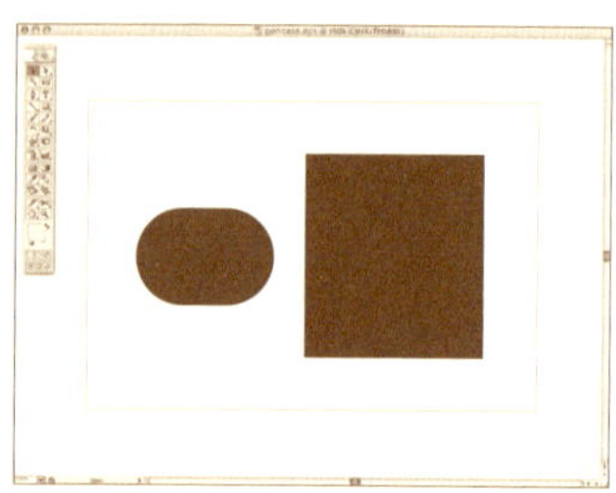

1

1. Open the mount data

Find the "pencase.eps" file in the "Template" folder in the attached CD-ROM. Copy it on to your hard disk, and open it with Illustrator. In the mount, you'll find two objects: one for the lid and another for the case.

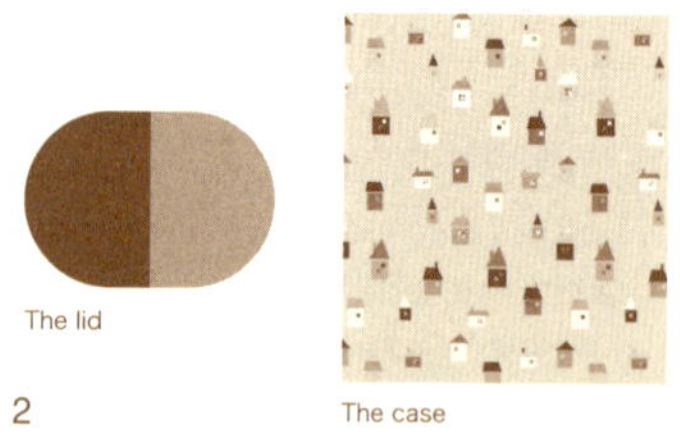

The lid

2

The case

2. Tile with the pattern

Thinking over the combinations of the colors and the patterns of the lid and the case as well as of the outer side and the reverse side, register the patterns you have chosen in "Swatch" (see p.181). Click on the "Select" tool and select the object on the document. Select the pattern which you have saved to paint the selected object. Now the data are ready to use.

3

3. Print on the canvas cloth and cut out

Set the cloth in the printer and print the design out. Here, we're using canvas with a covering of PET film on the back. (NB: all cloth for printing has a printing side. Stick to the detailed settings in the manual for the product you are using). Cut off the blank part all round and peel off the PET film on the back.

4

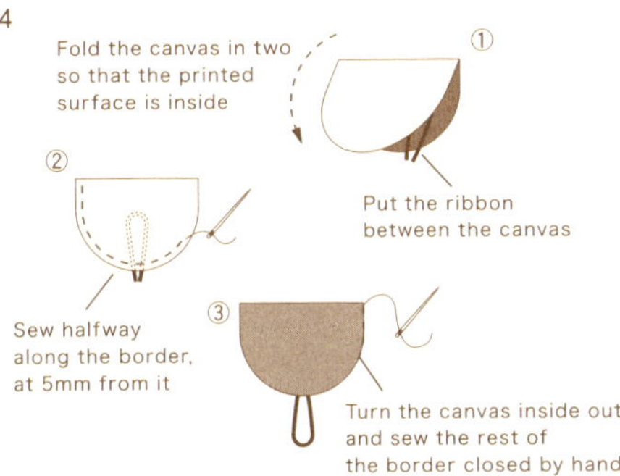

5

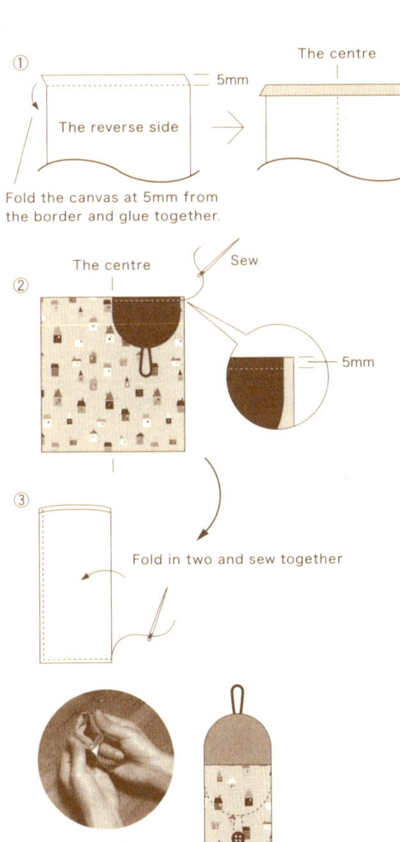

6

4. Make the lid

Firstly, make the lid of the case: ①Turn the canvas for the lid inside out and fold it in two. ②Put the ribbon between the canvas and sew along the border at 5mm from it. ③Turn the canvas inside out and sew the rest of the border closed by hand.

5. Sew the lid on to the case

Next, sew the lid on to the case: ①Fold the upper border of the canvas for the case at 5 mm from the edge and glue together. Once the glue has dried completely, fold the canvas in two to make a crease at the centre. ②Carefully place, printed side out, the upper border of the lid on to the upper border of the case as shown in the figures on the left and sew together at 5 mm from the edge. ③Fold the case in two and sew up the remaining three sides.

6. Sew on the button

Turn the case inside out, check the ribbon's location and sew on the button. Close the lid to check that the button is sewn on in the best place.

Now you have your own original pencase!

Petit Pattern Book: Kids & Toys
License Agreement of the Software

1. License

1) This License Agreement is a legal agreement between you (the "User"), who purchased the product Petit Pattern Book: Kids & Toys, and BNN, Inc. ("BNN"),. in respect of the attached CD-ROM entitled Petit Pattern Book: Kids & Toys ("Software"). The User agrees to be bound by the terms of this License Agreement by installing, copying, or using the Software. BNN grants the User the right to use a copy of the Software on one personal computer for the exclusive use of the User.

2) The User may modify, edit, or combine the materials included in the Software except the cases specified in "2. Limitations" ; the User has the right to use the Software principally for design of the following objects.
 ○Digital media including websites.
 ○Use them as a graphic tool for creating shop interiors, signs, or for free wrapping services at the counter.
 ○Leaflets, flyers, posters, direct mail, catalogues, pamphlets, and other tools for advertisement or sales promotion.
 ○Goods, clothes, greeting cards, name cards and other articles for personal production and use. (The Software may be used for personal, professional, and commercial purposes, provided that the articles produced are not offered for sale. The User may not sell articles made with the Software, even when of a personal nature. Please read the following Limitations carefully.)

2. Limitations

The User is not licensed to do any of the following:

1) Copy the Software, unless copying it is unavoidable to enable it to be used on one personal computer.
2) License, or otherwise by any means permit, any other person to use the Software.
3) Use the Software to design of products for distribution(for printed matter on sale, e.g. books and magazines).
4) For wrapping merchandise or paid gift-wrapping services.
5) As a part of the brand image of a company (even when this is still under consideration for the future).
6) Use the Software for the commercial production of postcards, name cards, or any other articles, or sell any such articles made using the Software.
7) Provide downloading services using the Software (including greeting card services).
8) Create an environment which allows the original data to be downloaded when you show one of the Software patterns on a home page.
9) Use the Software in order to produce any software or other products for sale.
10) Acquire the copyright in any material in the Software or any object you have created using the Software.
11) Use the Software to create obscene, scandalous, abusive or slanderous works.

We will be more than happy to discuss your needs with you if you are interested in using our materials for commercial designs or product sales. Please contact us on the following number.
○2m09cmGRAPHICS, Inc. (fax : +81-3-3470-2356 e-mail : info@209g.com)

3. Copyright and other intellectual property

BNN or its suppliers reserves the copyright and other intellectual property rights in the Software. When specifying the User's copyright of a product made using the Software, please also write "©2007 2m09cmGRAPHICS, Inc.".

4. Exclusion of damages

In no event shall BNN be liable for any damages whatsoever (including but not limited to, damages for loss of profit or loss of data) related to the use or inability to use of the Software or use of materials in the Software.

5. Termination of this License Agreement

If the User breaches this License Agreement, BNN has the right to withdraw the User's License granted on the basis hereof.

おしゃれなパターン素材集
Petit Pattern Book

水玉・ストライプ
Dots & Stripes
ISBN：4-86100-384-9

花柄・リーフ
Flowers & Leaves
ISBN：978-4-86100-385-1

北欧・ファブリック
Scandinavian Style
ISBN：978-4-86100-386-8

和・きもの柄
Japanese Style
ISBN：978-4-86100-390-5

チェック・ニット
Check & Knit
ISBN：978-4-86100-507-7

シンプル・ナチュラル
Simple & Natural
ISBN：978-4-86100-522-0

ポップ・モダン
Pop & Modern
ISBN：978-4-86100-523-7

秋・冬
Autumn & Winter
ISBN：978-4-86100-542-8

おしゃれなパターン素材集

キッズ・トイ

2007年1月25日　初版第1刷発行
2007年10月20日　初版第2刷発行

アートディレクション　中山正成（2m09cmGRAPHICS）

ブックデザイン　山際昇太（2m09cmGRAPHICS）

パターンデザイン　2m09cmGRAPHICS

翻訳　R.I.C.出版株式会社

発行人　籔内康一

発行所　株式会社ビー・エヌ・エヌ新社
〒104-0042
東京都中央区入船3-7-2　35山京ビル
fax 03-5543-3108　e-mail info@bnn.co.jp

印刷・製本　株式会社 シナノ

Printed in Japan
ISBN　978-4-86100-506-0